INFORMATION MODELLING

To my parents,
Patrick and Mary,
with love (D.J.F.)

To Guillemo, Elisa
and Miguel Angel (O.F.D.)

INFORMATION MODELLING
An international perspective

Donal J. Flynn and Olivia Fragoso Diaz

Department of Computation, University of Manchester
Institute of Science and Technology

PRENTICE HALL

*London   New York   Toronto   Sydney   Tokyo   Singapore
Madrid   Mexico City   Munich*

First published 1996 by
Prentice Hall Europe
Campus 400, Maylands Avenue
Hemel Hempstead
Hertfordshire, HP2 7EZ
A division of
Simon & Schuster International Group

Typeset in 10 on 12 pt Times
by Photoprint, Torquay, Devon

Printed and bound in Great Britain by
Redwood Books, Trowbridge, Wiltshire

Library of Congress Cataloging-in-Publication Data

Flynn, Donal J. (Donal James)
    Information modelling : an international perspective / Donal Flynn and
Olivia Fragoso Diaz.
        p.   cm.
    Includes bibliographical references and index.
    ISBN 0-13-234691-5 (pbk.)
    1. System design.   2. Information technology–Mathematical models.
I. Fragoso Diaz, Olivia.   II. Title.
QA76.9.S88F577   1995
005.1'2–dc20   95-31090
                                                                          CIP

British Library Cataloguing in Publication Data

A catalogue record for this book is available from
the British Library

ISBN 0–13–234691–5 (pbk)

---

1 2 3 4 5   00 99 98 97 96

CONTENTS

Part III Process model   119

Part V Conclusions

ABOUT THE AUTHORS

Donal Flynn has worked for 25 years in industry and academia for a variety of companies both at home and abroad, such as IBM (UK), National Westminster Bank, Rank Xerox and American Express in the UK, the Philips group in the Netherlands and Esso in Belgium. He has held a variety of roles, such as programmer, systems analyst, database designer, project manager and consultant.

At the Department of Computation in UMIST he is currently a senior lecturer in Information Systems. His research interests are in requirements engineering, strategic planning, user participation and in working with users as well as system designers to improve the process of modelling user requirements in organisations.

Olivia Fragoso Diaz graduated in Informatics from the Technological Institute of Durango, Mexico, has worked as a systems analyst for several companies, and recently completed research in information systems development methods in the Department of Computation at UMIST.

PREFACE

INFORMATION MODELLING

Information modelling is an important activity in computer-based information systems development. An information model concerns part of an organisation and its environment, representing the elements about which information is to be recorded and the way in which the information is to be processed.

Information models commonly take the form of entity-relationship models, data flow diagrams and entity life histories. The information model is checked by users to make sure that their requirements for the information system have been captured correctly and completely, and it is used later to design the information processing component of the information system for that organisation.

In this book, our examples are based on commercial and administrative information systems.

MOTIVATION

Need for standardisation

The motivation that has led to the development of this book is the steady progress that is being made towards standardisation in the area of information modelling.

The standardisation process has been assisted by the emergence of national, *de facto* standards for information systems development methods in several European countries. As internationalism extends its boundaries it is becoming more likely, for example, that a system intended for one country may have different parts built in several different countries. Where such co-operation is required the need for communication and eventual standardisation between different project teams and organisations is evident.

Another reason for this trend is the increasing importance being placed on system quality, reusability and re-engineering. It is no longer the case that software is the only product of any significance from the systems development process, and the importance of a high-level specification of requirements has increasingly been recognised as being linked to the existence of high-quality systems.

Information models of the organisation often feature strongly as part of such a specification of requirements. The drive towards reusing parts of existing systems, or re-engineering the organisation towards a future, more effective, state, is very difficult without the existence of such models. If the models exist in a standard form, then communication can clearly be improved between users, who need to make business decisions, and systems developers, who need to make technical decisions within a business context.

There is increasing pressure from users on software suppliers to improve the quality of information systems, and this has manifested itself in the TickIT scheme in the UK and the Capability Maturity Model in the US, whereby software suppliers can have their systems development process evaluated with respect to a standard. In addition, there are moves towards European or international standards for systems development such as Euromethod, Spice and ISO/IEC 12207.

We may briefly note two broad types of method standardisation. *Convergence* concerns a movement from diverse, existing methods to 'one best method', while *harmonisation* implies the existence of a reference method with which existing methods have explicit correspondences. However, if the result of convergence is at a sufficiently high level it may be equivalent to harmonisation.

Euromethod

A public sign of the acknowledgement of the trend towards standardisation is the movement exemplified by the Euromethod programme. The programme has evolved from a proposal made in May 1989 by European member states to the Commission of the European Communities. The proposal aimed to provide a reference framework for customers and software suppliers for use, in parallel with existing methods, as a basis for systems development.

The problem of the diversity of existing systems development methods is acknowledged, and a benefit that can be obtained from a standard 'Euromethod' is identified as facilitating communication among organisations which have adopted different methods and techniques. In addition, with an open European market, the use of Euromethod allows for easy bid comparisons when evaluating tenders for information systems, and can improve competition.

Further benefits are an increase in developer skills mobility, a reduction of problems resulting from, for example, misunderstandings due to different concept terminology, and the ability to retain existing methods.

AIMS

Main aims

Our first aim is to analyse and compare the information modelling capabilities of selected systems development methods to understand their similarities and differences, using a reference framework of common modelling concepts and viewpoints.

Our second aim is to show how such a reference framework may be used for method harmonisation by providing a basis for determining method correspondences.

The five methods we compare are Information Engineering (IE), Structured Systems Analysis and Design Method (SSADM), Metodologica Informatica (MEIN), MERISE, and Coad and Yourdon's Object-Oriented Analysis (OOA).

Our approach

We use a theoretical approach and a case study approach for a detailed discussion of method concepts and their meaning. For the theoretical approach, we use the reference framework to analyse method concepts, viewpoints, terminology, meanings and correspondences.

For the case study approach, we use the Aquaduct plumbing organisation as a case study to build information models for each of the methods. These models provide practical illustrations of the meaning and use of the concepts and viewpoints in the different diagrams provided by the methods, and allow an extra dimension of understanding, as they show the ways in which the concepts may be related together in a model.

Secondary aims

We establish whether the methods have a wide or narrow scope relative to one another and compare object-oriented with traditional methods.

We also provide outlines for developer guidance where there are modelling choices to be made and briefly indicate how these choices may be viewed as advantages or disadvantages, relative to a set of information modelling quality criteria. We do this to discuss the different situations which may favour or disfavour a particular modelling choice. Such guidance may form part of a future, more advanced reference framework.

In addition, to assist the understanding of method concepts and to show how they may be used in an integrated way, we discuss general principles for building information models, and also provide commentaries and principles that describe how we built the specific case study models.

Choice of methods

Traditional methods

Four of the five methods we compare are representative of the 'traditional' approach to systems development. This approach has been in wide use over the past twenty years and is the basis for the majority of software tools currently available to support system development.

Three of the methods, SSADM (UK), MERISE (France) and MEIN (Spain), were chosen as they are the most widely used methods in their respective European countries, while the fourth method, Information Engineering, has a wide international use. In addition, these methods are currently the subject of discussion in the Euromethod programme, are the most detailed with respect to information modelling, and are therefore the most suitable for our comparison, bearing in mind our aim to contribute towards method harmonisation.

The main references employed are: IE (Martin 1990); MEIN (MEIN II 1991); MERISE (Tardieu *et al.* 1983, 1985; Rochfeld and Tardieu 1983; Rochfeld 1987; Collongues *et al.* 1989; Planche 1992; Quang and Chartier-Kastler 1991); SSADM Version 4, (SSADM 1990). Several reference sources are used for MERISE as there are slightly different versions. Other SSADM sources used are Downs *et al.* (1992), Duschl and Hopkins (1992) and Hares (1990).

Our comparison only considers the information modelling part of the methods, which is typically in an early phase concerned with analysing user requirements.

Object-oriented methods

Object-oriented methods have emerged recently, claiming certain advantages over the traditional approach. To examine these claims, the fifth method we compare is Object-Oriented Analysis (OOA) (Coad and Yourdon 1991), a well-known object-oriented method for information modelling.

POTENTIAL READERS

We have aimed the book at the student, the practitioner and the researcher.

Student

The undergraduate student will acquire *knowledge* in terms of modelling concepts and terminology, and will acquire the basis for modelling *skills* by studying the case study models and understanding how they are built. To fully acquire modelling skills the authors recommend that the student attend a later or parallel module with a strong practical element in model building.

In addition, the reference framework presents the notion of a set of basic modelling concepts which will guide the student through the 'jungle' of methods, providing correspondences between the framework and the methods, and will provide knowledge concerning a broad range of methods.

The student who is following a computer science undergraduate course will find the contents at about the level of the second or third years, and will be of interest if they are attending both lecture-based and practical modules on information systems, systems analysis, data bases or information modelling. Knowledge of a systems development method is not a prerequisite but previous exposure to basic information systems concepts would be useful.

Those students who are following a course such as business studies or management, with a leaning towards information technology, will find the book useful for information concerning method harmonisation, method evolution and modelling issues in systems development.

Postgraduate students will find the reference framework and quality criteria for information modelling of use in their research.

Practitioner

For the practitioner, who already possesses modelling knowledge and skills, the usefulness of the book lies mainly in the fact that it presents the reference framework. With this framework we present a clear description of how the basic modelling concepts in each method are used to build information models from a business-oriented case study. This has three purposes. Firstly, it enables the meaning of the concepts to be clearly understood in the context of a practical example. Secondly, it provides a means to evaluate the scope of each of the methods against one another.

Thirdly, looking to the future, it provides a guide to the correspondences between methods, to address the situation where knowledge of different, widely used methods will be important in, for example, making and comparing bids for European systems development projects.

We also compare traditional approaches to information modelling with the more recent object-oriented approach, commenting on the underlying differences between the approaches as well as on the particular methods used in the comparison. This should be particularly interesting to those who acquired their modelling skills in the 'pre-object' era.

Student and practitioner

The methods display important variations, particularly for the modelling of processes, and we expect that both types of reader will profit from this fact by becoming aware of the different possibilities in this area, and by perhaps trying out a style that is different to their normal one. This might help everyone to become better at modelling!

We have written the book on the basis of our experience in both the practitioner and academic spheres. Our experience as practitioners has enabled us to choose realistic examples to illustrate the modelling concepts, while our experience as academics, based on the work of previous writers, many of whom are referenced in the bibliography, has helped us to define the reference framework concepts for analysing and comparing the important modelling features of the methods.

Researcher

For the researcher the main focus of interest is the reference framework we employ, the meanings of its concepts and viewpoints, and the correspondences of the methods to the framework. As the trend to standardisation proceeds, debate as to the scope and contents of reference frameworks will become increasingly common.

WHAT DOES AN INFORMATION MODEL MODEL?

We have expressed this question in a rather confusing way to draw attention to the fact that answers to the question may be confusing as well!

There are various positions that you may adopt when deciding what is to be modelled, and the position you choose will probably depend on your view of the nature of reality, which is termed your ontological view.

In the context with which we are concerned, the view of *naive realism* is that organisations are objective phenomena which exist independently of, and are perceived in the same way by, any observer, and an information model is thus a model of this objective reality.

Towards the other end of the ontological spectrum is what we may term the view of *subjectivism*, which is that an organisation is a phenomenon whose 'reality' is a product of an observer's perceptions of it and hence is unique for every observer; there is thus no objective reality and an information model is a model of the perceptions of one or more observers of 'the' organisation.

Both of these views are rather extreme, and the view in this book is that of *social constructivism*. This views organisations as socially constructed phenomena, whose many aspects may be perceived differently by different observers, but which are able, by negotiation, discussion or some other method, to formulate a common view for a period of time, containing a minimum of inconsistencies, that may be used as a basis for building an information model.

We close this short description of an important topic by stating an important assumption that we make: that the process of arriving at the common view of the organisation has taken place before the information modelling activity commences and that this common view is available to that activity.

CONTENTS AND STRUCTURE

The book is divided into five parts, where Part I, consisting of Chapter 1, defines the concept of method and describes several related topics. The Aquaduct plumbing organisation is then described, which we use as the central case study for all examples of modelling concepts.

Part II of the book presents the structure modelling part of the traditional methods, and Chapter 2 presents concepts related to entity and attribute, Chapter 3 describes concepts related to relationship, including cardinality and participation constraints, while Chapter 4 discusses multiple relationship modelling, with variations in cardinality and participation constraints.

In Chapter 5 concepts related to generalisation, aggregation and rule are described. In Chapter 6, the case study solution is presented, consisting of a structure model expressed in each of the methods, accompanied by a discussion of the principles used to build the models. Finally, Chapter 7 presents method correspondences and scope for structure modelling.

Part III of the book is concerned with process modelling. Chapter 8 describes the MEIN and SSADM process modelling concepts, and Chapter 9 contains the process models for the case study solution, expressed in the data flow diagrams of SSADM and MEIN, as well as a data dictionary and a full discussion of how to build the process model and the data dictionary.

Chapter 10 then describes IE and MERISE process modelling concepts and viewpoints and Chapters 11 and 12 show IE and MERISE process models for the case study. In the last chapter of this part, Chapter 13, we present method correspondences for process modelling and discuss method scope.

In Part IV, Chapter 14 discusses the concepts of Coad and Yourdon OOA and then discusses an OOA model for part of the case study. We describe OOA in one chapter as structure and process concepts are closely integrated. We compare the OOA model to the models of the traditional methods and draw conclusions concerning the differences between traditional and object-oriented approaches to information modelling.

Finally in Part V, Chapter 15 draws the main conclusions, considering method correspondences in terms of the reference framework, method scope and 'softer' issues such as modelling guidance and approaches to process grouping that differentiate OOA from the traditional approaches, closing with remarks on the progress to be made towards method harmonisation. The appendix contains a summary of the reference framework.

We would like to particularly acknowledge fruitful discussions on the meanings of method concepts which we had with Alberto Laender and David Knight. The anonymous referees also provided many helpful insights and comments which have helped to improve the book a great deal.

ABBREVIATIONS AND ACRONYMS

BS	British Standard
BSI	British Standards Institute
CASE	Computer-aided software (or systems) engineering
CCTA	Central Computing and Telecommunications Agency
CMM	Capability Maturity Model
CPM	Conceptual Processing Model
CRIS	Comparative review of information systems
DDSS	Development of data sharing systems
DFD	Data flow diagram
DSDM	Dynamic systems development method
EC	European Community
ELH	Entity life history
ER	Entity-relationship
FD	Flow diagram
IE	Information Engineering
IEC	International Electrotechnical Commission
IS	Information System
ISO	International Standards Organisation
JSD	Jackson System Development
LDS	Logical data structure
MEIN	Metodologica Informatica
OO	Object-oriented
OOA	Object-oriented analysis
OOD	Object-oriented design
OOP	Object-oriented programming
RAD	Rapid application development
SPICE	Software process improvement and capability determination
SSADM	Structured systems analysis and design method
STRADIS	Structured analysis, design and implementation of information systems
UK	United Kingdom
US	United States
YSM	Yourdon Structured Method

Part I

METHODS AND CASE STUDY

In Part I we discuss several introductory topics concerning methods which help to place information modelling in context, and we then present the case study of the Aquaduct plumbing organisation.

We begin by giving some definitions of important terms, such as method, method phase, product and model and then describe what methods aim to do, within a context of information systems quality and productivity. We remark on the fact that there are many methods in existence and then show the main points in the evolution of methods over the past 25 years, briefly describing the typical activities in the phases of current, data-oriented methods.

The traditional and object-oriented methods that we study are then located within our evolutionary description, and their main phases briefly described. The general type of activities in the information modelling part of the methods which is our focus of comparison are then described in more detail.

We then consider whether methods have met the aims presented earlier, summarising their advances and then listing problems found that concern information modelling. After a very brief survey of wider problems found with methods, and a consideration of the types of improvements currently being made, we discuss the issue of method standards. Several standards in this area are listed and we finish by discussing the convergence and harmonisation approaches to standardisation.

Part I closes with a description of the Aquaduct case study.

Chapter 1

METHODS AND AQUADUCT CASE STUDY

The aim of this chapter is to discuss various topics concerning systems development methods and then to introduce the Aquaduct case study.

DEFINITIONS AND TERMINOLOGY

Method

A *systems development method*, or *method*, may be defined as follows:

> A method is an integrated set of activities and products for the specification or generation of an information system.

The process of applying a method to develop an information system is termed the *systems development process*.

The definition refers to specification or generation as some methods do not cover all of the systems development process, and only produce specifications rather than actual systems.

There are several terms in use which are broadly equivalent to method, such as methodology, development method, systems development method and approach, in this context. A technique is usually more specific, referring to a well-defined task which addresses a particular area of the development process.

Phases and products

To reduce the complexity of a method it is usually split up into different *phases*, consisting of activities and smaller tasks. Activities and phases generate *products*, which may be, for example, a description of a user requirement, part of a specification, a piece of program code or an operational system.

Model, modelling and modelling concept

A model may be defined generally as *an abstract representation of a part of reality*.

We shall use the term *model* to refer to an abstract representation of a part of an organisation that constitutes a product of the information modelling part of a method. It is common for such models to include aspects of the organisational environment.

The term *modelling* refers to the activity of building a model, while a *modelling concept* is a conceptual 'building block' that is used to build a model and that is provided by the information modelling part of a method.

We should point out that the term 'model' may be used in many different ways in the information systems literature.

THE AIMS OF METHODS

In general, methods aim to produce information systems which possess the characteristics of high *quality* and *productivity*. The concept of high quality is that a system should meet the requirements of all its users, while that of high productivity is that the system should be developed on time and on budget.

A poor quality system may fall into disuse or may be sabotaged; it will be a waste of the organisation's resources and may even have the effect of putting the organisation out of business if it affects a critical area. A system developed with poor productivity may invalidate its cost–benefit justification if it costs more than planned, or may miss a business opportunity if it is developed too late.

METHOD PROLIFERATION

Figure 1.1 shows the main methods developed by practitioners over the past 25 years. These are described in detail in Hares (1990), who describes how the MODUS and DDSS methods, developed by the software houses BIS and CACI respectively, have led to two of the most widely used methods in the UK, SSADM and Information Engineering.

Other streams discussed are structured methods developed in the United States such as STRADIS and the Yourdon Structured Method (YSM), as well as methods focused on real-time applications and object-oriented methods. Finally, there are the major national methods used within the European Community countries.

In addition, there are methods which have been developed mainly by researchers, and many are described in the Comparative Review of Information Systems (CRIS) series of books which analyse and review methods (Olle *et al.* 1982,

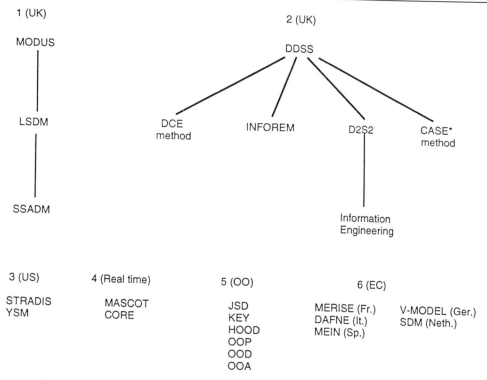

Figure 1.1 Methods and their development (adapted from J. Hares, *SSADM for the advanced practitioner*, Wiley, Chichester, 1990). © 1990 John Wiley & Sons Ltd. Reprinted by permission of John Wiley & Sons Ltd.

1983, 1986, 1988; Verrijn-Stuart and Olle 1994) and which have encouraged debate and interaction between practitioners and researchers.

METHOD EVOLUTION

The proliferation of so many methods has led to the situation where there is a method 'jungle'. To try to 'hack' our way through this jungle we may look at the way in which methods have evolved.

Early era (pre-1970)

In this period, only analysis and programming activities were identified. User requirements were analysed into program specifications by systems analysts who passed these to programmers to produce code. The activities were only loosely defined and the program flowchart was almost the only standard product in use.

The activity emphasised was programming, as program execution efficiency, in terms of either execution speed or main memory size, was the overriding consideration, due to hardware limitations. An example of a method of this type in the UK was that recommended by the National Computing Centre, described in Daniels and Yeates (1969).

Structured methods – 1970s

Structured programming

The activities of the programming phase gradually became more defined, due partly to the central principle that only three constructs – sequence, selection and iteration – were sufficient to code programs with one entry and exit point (Bohm and Jacopini 1966; Dijkstra 1968).

Testing, termed code inspection (Fagan 1976), was distinguished from programming by instituting a walkthrough procedure, with defined activities and individuals, to check code before it was tested by execution.

Structured design

Program design techniques appeared which distinguished physical design from programming activities, and there were two main approaches, the functional and the data structured approach.

In the *functional approach*, Stevens *et al.* (1974) proposed the decomposition of a system into a number of hierarchical functions or modules, showing these on a structure chart and applying coupling and cohesion rules to guide the design. Data flow diagrams were used to identify major data transformations and sub-systems and to act as a basis for the production of structure charts.

In the *data structured approach* (Jackson 1975; Warnier 1974), the structure of input and output data, shown diagrammatically in a structure chart, was used to determine program structure in terms of its hierarchical functions.

Structured analysis

This distinguished the phase of analysis from design, aiming to provide a non-technical description of user requirements. It focused on the data flow diagram (DFD) (De Marco 1979; Gane and Sarson 1979; Yourdon and Constantine 1979), which modelled the requirements in terms of a hierarchical decomposition of processes and data flows, rather than the programs and files of the design phase. The highest-level data flow diagram gave an overview of the system for clarification of requirements. Also provided were facilities for more detailed specification, such as minispecifications, decision tables, decision trees and a data dictionary.

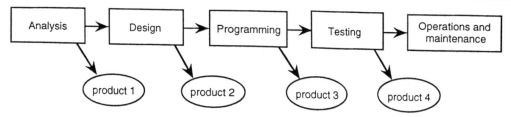

Figure 1.2 Avalanche model of systems development.

Avalanche model

These phases and products were described by a general model of systems development, shown in Figure 1.2, termed the avalanche model, as more and more detail was added progressively through subsequent phases, creating an increasing volume of documentation.

The separation between phases was important as it established the concept of *abstraction*. Early phases and their products were on a high level of abstraction, focusing on *what* the user requirements were, and abstracted away from lower-level phases, which were concerned with *how* the requirements were to be implemented.

Data-oriented methods – 1980s

Structured methods assumed that users only wanted to computerise a current, manual system for efficiency gains. However, new systems were needed that often required significant user involvement and discussion. This brought about an emphasis on the analysis phase.

In addition, structured methods were process oriented, with the effect that specifications were often too detailed and computer oriented for users to understand.

Data orientation

This emphasised the modelling of data or objects, using entity modelling or normalisation techniques. It had the effect of distinguishing the analysis phase more clearly, as, by considering objects in isolation from processes, it was more abstract and encouraged new ways to think about the organisation.

User orientation

There was a growing realisation that many systems did not meet user requirements, and this was addressed in two ways. Firstly, it was necessary to involve users more actively in the process so that they could check the specification. Hence, products were made easier for them to understand, and iteration was introduced into systems development, allowing phases to incorporate changes.

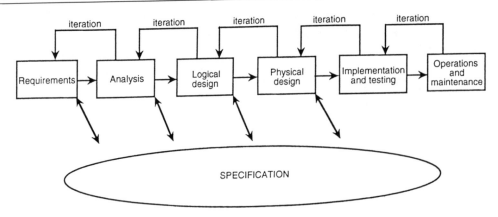

Figure 1.3 *Iterative model of systems development.*

Secondly, a greater range of activities for determining user requirements emerged, such as strategic planning and cost–benefit determination, which were useful for the newer types of systems referred to above.

Iterative model

The avalanche model of systems development had evolved into an iterative model, as shown in Figure 1.3. Iteration was incorporated between one or more phases, and the emphasis on abstraction and the early phases led to the emergence of a specific requirements phase. The different products shown in Figure 1.2 were now part of a more integrated specification.

Iterative model phases

The typical activities in each phase may be described as follows:

- *Requirements*. Elicit and capture requirements from users.

- *Analysis*. Analyse user requirements in detail and express them precisely in the specification, retaining user terms and avoiding computer-oriented detail.

  This phase is primarily concerned with information modelling activities, which build an information model of the relevant part of the organisation and environment, focusing on the elements about which information is to be recorded, the elements which send and receive information and the way in which information is to be processed.

- *Logical design*. The specification is used to produce a design for a computer-based system that will serve as the basis for the implemented information system. Often, the interaction between the human and the computer system is designed here.

- *Physical design.* The logical design is targeted on hardware, software, human and organisational components.

- *Implementation and testing.* The system is implemented in software and human procedures and is tested.

- *Operations and maintenance.* Operations consists of the system in operation in the organisation while maintenance consists of the activities which request and make changes to the system.

METHODS CONSIDERED IN THIS BOOK

Traditional methods

Four of the methods that we consider, Information Engineering, SSADM, MEIN and MERISE, are all examples of the data-oriented type of method, and Figure 1.4 shows their main phases.

We are primarily interested in their information modelling activities and these are all located in the analysis phase, as described above. Information modelling is important as it produces a specification of the information and its processing that

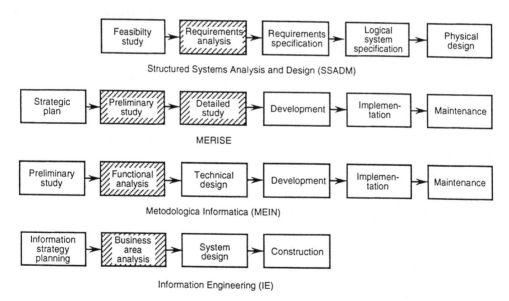

Figure **1.4**   *Main phases of Information Engineering, SSADM, MERISE and MEIN.*

will be part of the information system. All methods have a preceding phase where requirements are determined, and a succeeding phase where the specification is used for logical design.

Object-oriented methods

In the later part of the book, we compare an object-oriented (OO) method, Object-Oriented Analysis (Coad and Yourdon 1991), to the four data-oriented methods, which we term 'traditional' methods.

The OO approach has evolved from early OO programming languages such as Simula in 1967 and Smalltalk in the 1970s, with Object Pascal, Ada and C++ as more recent examples of object-oriented programming; principles for modular specification (Parnas 1972) and work on the design level may be found in Jackson System Development (JSD) (Jackson 1983).

The more recent application of OO principles to the design and analysis levels of systems development has resulted in object-oriented design (OOD), as exemplified by Booch (1991), and object-oriented analysis (OOA), as presented in Coad and Yourdon (1991), Shlaer and Mellor (1988) and Rumbaugh *et al.* (1991). From database design the work of Chen (1976) with the entity relationship (ER) model and Brodie with transaction analysis (Brodie and Silva 1982) has also been influential.

OO methods emerged into wide use in the late 1980s and are usually focused on particular phases. For example, object-oriented analysis, object-oriented design and object-oriented programming focus on the analysis, design and implementation and testing phases respectively.

We chose Coad and Yourdon OOA for comparison as it is on the analysis level, being mainly concerned with building an information model. Object-oriented methods are of particular interest to our comparison as they propose a different paradigm for information modelling. Their aim is similar to data-oriented methods as their focus is on objects or data, but they group processes by the object on which those processes operate.

We shall see in the comparison later that the traditional methods have a variety of ways for grouping processes, and do not integrate process with object so tightly.

INFORMATION MODELLING

Information modelling builds the information model, which usually consists of two main components, the structure model and the process model.

The structure model describes the organisational and environmental elements about which information is to be recorded, commonly using the concepts of entity, attribute and relationship and showing these on an entity-relationship diagram.

The process model describes the elements concerned with processing the information, using concepts such as process, event and data flow and expressing these in terms of structure model elements. Process models can be, for example, data flow diagrams, process decompositions or entity life histories.

There may be a third component to the information model, the rule model, which restricts the values of elements in the structure model, but its scope and contents are presently a research issue which we shall not cover here.

The information model is on a conceptual level, so the data that will be recorded concerning the structure model entities, attributes and relationships will not be decided until later on in the design phases of systems development, where the processes will also be designed to operate on this data rather than on structure model elements.

SUMMARY OF METHOD EVOLUTION

Figure 1.5 shows the evolution of methods in terms of the systems development phase they emphasise. The figure shows that the trend in emphasis is to the requirements phase. However, this is occurring at a slower rate than the movement through the programming and design phases. OO methods have not made a contribution to this trend, but have instead proposed the object-oriented paradigm for the later phases.

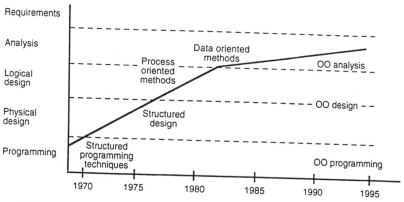

Figure 1.5 *Method development in terms of emphasis on systems development phases.*

DO METHODS MEET THEIR AIMS?

Method improvements

We now summarise the ways in which methods have evolved to achieve the aims of high quality and productivity.

- Phases and their activities have become more clearly defined, replacing developer intuition by guidance and allowing the process to be better managed. This should reduce developer error.

- Products have been defined more clearly so that user requirements can be modelled correctly and precisely in all the detail required. They have become simpler so that developers make fewer errors and users can understand them and check that their requirements are modelled correctly.

- The early phases have become more abstract, facilitating user involvement, leading to more accurate definition and capture of user requirements and also helping requirements checking.

- Object-oriented methods promise a smoother transition between the different phases, as the object-oriented paradigm is used throughout.

Problems found

There have been many reports of problems and failures of information systems (Flynn 1992). Some studies, for example Eason (1988), report that only 20 per cent of systems may have a positive effect on organisations.

It is difficult to say whether the evolution in methods has improved the quality and productivity of information systems. This is because the systems developed today are very much more complex than those developed in the early 1970s, making a comparison difficult, and because there are many factors, other than the method used, which affect the eventual system.

We shall discuss only those problems that relate to the information modelling part of methods, concerning the high quality aim of methods. Common problems are as follows:

- Methods vary in their scope and some cannot model all aspects of requirements.

- A terminology problem exists as methods can use different terms for the same concept and the same terms for different concepts, confusing developers and users.

- A basic set of modelling concepts has not been agreed upon, so it is not possible to provide good developer guidance for either activities or products. Modelling errors may thus easily be made.

- Models are often expressed in a form that is difficult for users to understand, making validation ineffective and leading to a poor quality system.

In the last section of this chapter we shall show how we can address some of these problems.

MORE RECENT METHODS AND PROBLEMS ADDRESSED

Our short survey of methods and their evolution would be incomplete without reference to more recent methods. We have a relatively narrow focus in this book, as we study only the information modelling part of methods. In addition, the type of methods we consider are what may be termed 'hard' or 'technical' methods. Such methods focus only on the computer-based aspect of the eventual system and neglect the 'soft' or more human-related aspects of systems.

Wider criticisms

Many criticisms and suggestions for method improvement are concerned with identifying different types of methods (Hirschheim and Klein 1989) or improving 'hard' methods by changing them into 'soft' methods.

Examples of the wider type of method criticism are the following:

- Methods assume requirements are fixed and are all known at the start of the development process. However, it is well known that requirements change as development proceeds, due to environmental factors, or to users learning more about technology or their organisation.

- Methods focus on the wrong problem in the organisation, providing a system that is not really needed, or do not allow sufficient user involvement for requirements to be defined correctly and completely and specifications validated.

- Methods emphasise the technical aspects of information systems only, neglecting the more human social and psychological context into which systems must be integrated.

- Methods take too much time as developers focus on relatively unimportant exercises such as detailed form-filling.

Criticisms addressed

To cope with the criticisms above, new or improved methods constantly appear, and in this section we will give you a flavour of some of these, indicating the criticisms at which they are targeted.

Changing requirements

The evolutionary approach (Crinnion 1991) is a method that suggests splitting a system into several parts, with each of these parts being developed separately, so that users have an opportunity to learn their requirements gradually. On a more general level, Boehm (1985) has proposed a spiral model of systems development which explicitly incorporates iteration.

Wrong problem/user involvement

For finding the key problem areas in an organisation critical success factors (Flynn and Arce, 1995) or organisational goal analysis (Yu 1993) may be used. The prototyping approach (Ramesh and Luqi 1993) suggests that user involvement and validation is best if users can see and experiment with an actual system instead of abstract specifications, and there are several methods which incorporate software tools to prototype part or all of a system.

Technical aspects only

The 'soft' methods address this area, and often cover a wide set of issues. There are methods which elicit and negotiate complex business requirements (Checkland 1981), often because the introduction of computer technology requires a radical reappraisal of business processes (Hammer 1990). Other methods aim to avoid negative social and psychological effects stemming from the introduction of an unfamiliar or unwanted technology (Mumford 1983; Harker *et al.* 1990). More specifically, some methods focus on the 'usability' of the eventual system for its users (Gould *et al.* 1991).

Too much time

Many methods are supported by CASE (computer aided software engineering) tools (Flynn *et al.* 1995), which manage large volumes of data and automate repetitive tasks in the development process.

STANDARDS

Trends

A more recent feature of method development is that steps have been taken towards standardisation. The sources for standardisation vary, and can be industry, an international standards authority or a body such as the European Commission. In addition, the scope of the standard can vary from a high-level overview of the systems development process to a detailed description of different types of product.

It is likely that standardisation will increase in the future, as it brings advantages such as reduced costs, simplified training and promises higher quality systems.

Existing standards

The UK standard BS 5750 (British Standards Institute 1987) and its equivalent, international standard ISO 9001, is a very general standard covering the management aspects of any manufacturing process, and many organisations require their suppliers to comply with this standard for the production of software.

The TickIT scheme (TickIT 1992), originally sponsored by the Department of Trade and Industry in the UK, is a certification process that is more specific to systems development. It assesses the quality management system of the systems development process in an organisation, applying the ISO 9001-3 standard which is targeted at the management aspects of software production.

In the US, the Capability Maturity Model (CMM), developed under the sponsorship of the Department of Defense (Humphrey 1989) defines five levels of maturity of the systems development process in an organisation. Each level of the model is characterised by certain properties which relate to the procedures used to manage the process. For example, a level 1 organisation possesses an *ad hoc* or chaotic systems development process, with no formal procedures or cost estimation mechanisms.

Euromethod

Overview

The current status of Euromethod (CCTA 1994; Franckson 1994) is concerned with defining the deliverables to be exchanged between customer and supplier during all aspects of systems development, from call for tendering to operational system (Jenkins 1992). However, the emphasis appears to be on the early rather than on the later stages of this process.

Seven methods were selected as the basis for the development of Euromethod: SSADM (UK), MERISE (France), SDM (Netherlands), DAFNE (Italy), Vorgehensmodell (Germany), MEIN (Spain) and Information Engineering.

Euromethod version 0 was delivered in June 1994 (EM 1994), and after a trialling period, version 1 is expected in 1996. Initially, it is expected to be used on advertised EC public procurement projects but it is unclear as to whether its use will be mandatory for such projects.

Deliverables

The deliverables are defined in terms of general concepts in the Deliverables Model, and consist of three main types: target domain, delivery plan and project domain deliverables.

Target domain deliverables relate to the information system to be developed and consist of IS-descriptions and operational items. The delivery plan describes the customer–supplier relationships during the development process, defining initial, final and in-between states of the organisation and information system and a sequence of decision points. Project domain deliverables relate to the development process and consist of project plans and project reports.

IS-descriptions

An IS-description describes elements of an information system and is equivalent in meaning to our notion of product. It may consist of one or more of six views which, in terms of IS-properties, describe different, though overlapping, sets of system elements. Together, the views define the concepts and terminology used to describe an information system.

Three views are information system views, and three are computer system views. The information system views define the representation of the information resource, the actors using and producing it and their processes with the relationships between them. They are the business information view, business process view and work practice view. The computer system views define the representation of the data, structure and functionality of the computer system. They are the computer system data view, computer system function view and computer system architecture view.

The information system views are all on the level of the analysis phase, as described above, and to give a flavour of their level of detail the business process view consists of the following IS-properties: business process, triggering events, triggering conditions, generated events, process decomposition, dynamic dependencies, business rules and information use.

Harmonisation

Euromethod sees two steps on the path to method harmonisation. Firstly, it describes, in the Method Bridging Guide, products and concepts of different European methods in terms of the concepts and IS-properties of the Deliverables Model, and secondly it foresees the situation where methods may converge their terminology towards Euromethod.

ISO/IEC standard 12207

This draft standard (Singh 1994) may be seen as a complement to Euromethod as it is not a documentation standard but instead defines the key processes in systems development. It does this with a high-level framework of modular processes which it does not sequence, leaving this decision to individual development projects. This is done so that the architecture shall be open and can be used with any model of systems development.

There are three broad types of process: primary, supporting and organisational, and they cover the key activities of roles such as supplier, acquirer, operator, maintainer and project manager. The architecture emphasises the principles of total quality management and emphasises the later activities in the development process, as twelve of the fourteen activities are concerned with system design or software.

Rapid application development – DSDM

The last example of an emerging standard we shall describe ('A radical step', *Computing*, 2 March 1995) is termed the Dynamic Systems Development Method (DSDM) and is a UK industry-generated standard for rapid application development (RAD). This is addressed at the criticism discussed above whereby systems development is often too slow. DSDM provides a high-level framework for developing systems founded on thirteen key principles. Two of these principles are that user involvement in RAD is imperative and iterative development and testing should be integrated through the life cycle.

HARMONISATION AND CONVERGENCE

Problems due to many methods

A well-known researcher (Bubenko 1986) states that many hundreds, and possibly thousands, of methods exist.

This is not a satisfactory situation for industry for several reasons. Organisations that wish to procure software are faced with many suppliers, each of whom may use a different method to develop software, making it difficult to understand what will eventually be delivered. Management have continual training costs when employing staff who may not be familiar with the method in use in their organisation, and programmers and analysts do not have a common language for communication, lack skills mobility and may not be receiving adequate guidance from the method they use.

For researchers, the situation is also not satisfactory as research effort is scattered over many methods and does not communicate owing to different terminology.

Convergence or harmonisation?

Convergence

Convergence implies a movement towards a common standard for methods, based on the notion of 'one best method', with the advantage that there would be only one method to deal with.

However, this approach has many disadvantages and we list three here. Firstly, in a market situation, it is not easy to see how competitive forces would allow such an advantage to be given to the method owner. Secondly, there is currently no general agreement, from industry or research, as to the best method. Thirdly, many organisations have substantial investments in their current methods, such as training and CASE tools.

Where convergence may work is in a new area, where organisational investment is slight or where no commercial advantage will obviously result to the owner of the standard. The TickIT and CMM schemes discussed above are examples of this. A market factor which may lead to convergence is pressure from organisations on their software suppliers to standardise aspects of systems development, and Quintas (1994) quotes the example of British Telecom, who required all their suppliers to have BS 5750 accreditation from the mid-1980s.

Harmonisation

Harmonisation implies firstly the development of a standard or reference framework which wins general acceptance in principle. The second step is not to remove existing methods but to establish method correspondences to the reference framework. Co-existence between reference framework and methods is thus the key factor of this approach.

Depending on the level of detail of the reference framework, the correspondences may be in terms of names of method phases or products, activities within phases, techniques or detailed products of activities.

An example of the effect of harmonisation in practice may be seen in the situation where a supplier uses a method to produce the deliverables required for a tender for a software contract. In this case, the deliverables would be supplemented by a description of their correspondences with the reference framework.

A third step towards harmonisation is similar to convergence, where methods gradually converge towards the reference framework. Harmonisation is of more recent origin than convergence and Euromethod is an example of the harmonisation approach. The disadvantages of harmonisation are that it requires an extra initial investment in the reference framework, it may be superseded by a technical or management advance, or the subject area may be too immature or diverse for a satisfactory reference framework to be constructed (Avison and Nandhakumar 1995).

Our view on harmonisation

The main aims of this book, as stated in the preface, are to support method harmonisation. We focus on the aspect of methods concerned with information modelling, which is a good subject for harmonisation as it is on an abstract level, independent of both the design and implementation issues of computer systems, as well as those activities and norms which are particular to specific organisations.

Our approach to harmonisation is to use a set of common modelling concepts and viewpoints, or perspectives on an organisation, which constitute a reference framework, to determine method correspondences between concepts, terminology, diagrams and viewpoints.

Based on this we point out whether the selected methods have a wide or narrow scope, and suggest the form that developer guidance should take where there are modelling choices to be made, using the notion of quality criteria. Our objective in doing this is not to establish which method is better than another, but to discuss the different situations or viewpoints which may favour or disfavour a particular modelling choice.

Our results will help to address three of the criticisms of information modelling in methods that we made above, concerning method variation in scope, the terminology problem and the fact that a common set of modelling concepts does not exist.

CASE STUDY

The Aquaduct case study is introduced in this chapter as it is the source of all the modelling examples in the book. It is a summarised account of an organisation and its environment and thus provides a welcome view on to the real world, to help offset the feeling of unreality which can often creep into the modelling process.

Although a description would not normally be structured as well as this in a typical systems development project, the advantage for this book is that the reader can easily understand the business or organisational context from which the examples have been drawn, without getting lost in a complex description.

AQUADUCT PLUMBING ORGANISATION

Jane Howard and Dave Bentham are the managing partners of the plumbing business Aquaduct. The business is a growing concern and it has recently been reorganised into separate departments, such as engineering, accounts, inventory, sales and marketing, some of which contain more than one section. The main focus of the business is carrying out water-related services for private and commercial customers. These include household repairs, pipework for new apartments, houses and offices, and complex projects involving water delivery, cooling and conservation systems for power generation plants.

(1) Potential or existing customers contact Aquaduct with their needs and, after ascertaining customer details, a job proposal is sent to them. On customer acceptance the proposal, or an amended version, becomes a job order, and a manager is assigned to the job order. Some job orders have several customers and a set of related job orders may be classed as a project.

(2) There are several types of employee, including managers, salespersons and security guards. Employee details including card number, names, address and telephone numbers are recorded; card number is unique and is mandatory, while the other details are optional; telephones are shared and several employees may have the same address. In addition, managers have a parking place number and salespersons have a sales club number. Security guards may be assigned to both buildings and car parks, but salespersons may be either telephone or direct salespersons. Customers are assigned to exactly two salespersons and employees work with other employees in teams.

(3) A customer holds an Aquaduct account for each relevant job order; the account belongs to the customer. Certain projects are very prestigious and the marketing department may plan an advertising campaign which publicises that project and the involvement of Aquaduct. Alternatively, a project may be

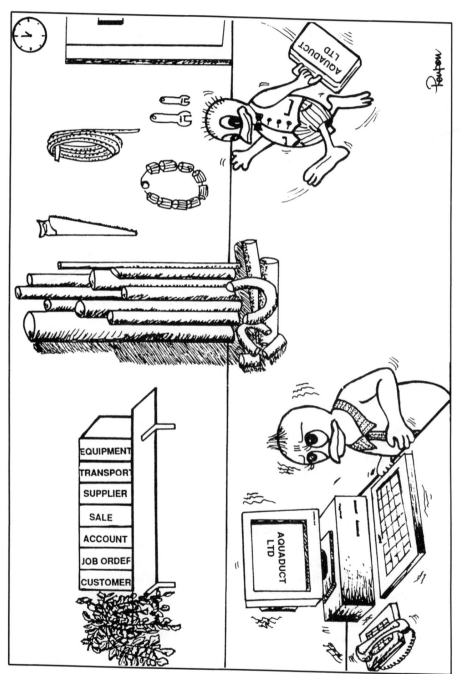

The Aquaduct Organisation.

publicised by sponsoring a local initiative, such as a school project or artistic festival, but it may not be publicised by both a campaign and an initiative. A campaign or initiative concern only one project and vice versa.

(4) A customer may be dissatisfied, as happens from time to time, and Aquaduct are proud of their complaints procedure which they set up to deal with this situation. This is described in the literature which is sent to every customer concerning a job order and involves a hotline telephone number for customers to phone. Complaints information recorded concerns the customer, the job order and the department concerned. Departments comprise sections and section names are unique only within their department.

(5) Apart from the benefit to customer relations provided by this procedure, Aquaduct find that complaints constitute a source of information that is useful for inducting new staff, as well as leading to reviews of organisation procedures. Information is recorded concerning presentations which may be made where managers talk about the experience of job orders with different customers. A manager can make a presentation about only one job order and one customer.

The activities that are carried out at the beginning and end of a job order, and those activities concerning payments, may be summarised as follows:

(6) *Job request.* Customers make job requests to Aquaduct, and in response the request may be rejected, or a job proposal may be written and sent to the customers. The customer may approve or reject the proposal. If it is rejected the proposal is closed.

(7) *Job proposal.* A job proposal must specify the parts needed, their prices and the cost of labour, obtained from the job costing section. The proposal is sent to the customer with a job order form. If the customer approves the proposal, the customer must sign the job order form and make the first payment for the job order. Aquaduct sends the proposal and a receipt for the first payment to the customer.

(8) *Job order.* When the job order is signed, the file of parts is checked. If parts are not in stock, indicated by the quantities, a purchase order is prepared and sent to an approved supplier. The date and time when a supplier was approved for a part is recorded. The supplier must supply bills and receipts for any supplied parts, which are used to update the supplier account. A supplier should have an account eventually, but not necessarily initially. The parts file is updated with any new parts.

(9) *Customer account.* When a job order is signed, the customer account is updated with customer details. At the end of the month a reminder is sent to a customer to pay a certain amount. On receipt of payment, the payment is checked against the customer account, which is then updated.

(10) When a job has finished and the customer has made all the payments, an end-of-job report will be sent to the customer. In addition, the account balance is elaborated and sent, along with customer details, to the accountant.

(11) *Supplier account.* The suppliers should send reminders every end of month to Aquaduct. Aquaduct checks the supplier account and, if valid, makes a payment to the supplier. The supplier account is updated. If the reminder amount is inconsistent with the supplier account, then the supplier account balance is elaborated and sent, along with supplier details, to the accountant.

(12) *Parts file.* At the end of every month, a report about transactions on parts is produced and sent to the accountant. If an error exists in the report it is redone. To monitor part quality, information may be kept for each part supplied by a supplier, recording ratings and the date of the ratings.

Part II

STRUCTURE MODEL

Part II discusses the concepts and diagrams provided by the four methods, Information Engineering, SSADM, MEIN and MERISE, for the structure model. We shall discuss the concepts in the methods and then present the structure model for the case study in Chapter 6, concluding with a method comparison in Chapter 7, where we summarise the correspondences between the methods and the reference framework and discuss major differences and method scope.

We will present and define each concept generally, and discuss the corresponding concept (if any) in each of the methods. To allow our concept definitions to be fairly succinct we will assume that the context is that of building an information model of part of an organisation.

Reference framework

The reference framework concepts for the structure model are: entity, attribute, identifier, attribute relationship constraints, binary relationship, cardinality constraint, participation constraint, relationship attribute, *n*-ary relationship, generalisation, property inheritance, multiple inheritance, exclusion, exhaustion, aggregation and rule.

Structure model components

Diagrams

The diagrams which comprise the structure models of the methods are as follows:

Information Engineering	Entity-relationship diagram
SSADM	Logical data structure (LDS)
MEIN	Entity-relationship diagram
MERISE	Conceptual data model (CDM)

Text

In addition, the methods suggest that the structure model should contain a description of all attributes in a textual form, which is separate from the diagram to avoid diagrammatic complexity. However, they do not describe this in sufficient detail, and so we use a common form, which we term the entity–attribute list, for all methods.

Chapter 2

ENTITY AND ATTRIBUTE

In this chapter we define the reference framework concepts concerning entities and attributes and analyse the corresponding concepts in the methods. The reference framework concepts used are entity, attribute, identifier and attribute relationship constraints.

All of the examples used are taken from the Aquaduct case study, and a complete structure model for each method can be found in Chapter 6.

ENTITY

Definition

An *entity* represents an object of interest in an organisation that may be concrete or abstract, and which is static rather than dynamic.

Let us consider the case of the Aquaduct plumbing organisation in the case study. In Aquaduct, for example, customers have customer accounts and suppliers supply parts. Here, customer, supplier, customer account and part are objects of interest to the organisation, where customer and supplier are concrete objects and customer account is an abstract object.

For a more precise definition we use the terms *entity type* and *entity instance*:

> An entity type represents a set or class of entities in an organisation that share the same characteristics.

> An entity instance represents a particular entity in an organisation that is a member of an entity set or class.

To avoid cumbersome terminology, we will follow normal practice and use the term entity to refer to an entity type.

This definition of entity is rather vague and does not really help when trying to identify entities in an organisation as part of building an information model. To

Instances of an entity share the same characteristics.

address the problem, we provide some principles and guidelines in Chapter 6 which are general in nature, but which also help you to understand how we arrived at the case study solution.

IE

For IE, 'entities are people, things or concepts that are of importance for the enterprise and about which we want to store information, they can be tangible or intangible' (Martin 1990).

The graphical representation of an entity in IE is a rectangular box with its name written inside. An example is shown in Figure 2.1.

Employee

Figure 2.1 Entity employee (IE).

IE also describes the intersection entity, which we do not discuss here as it is not conceptually different from a normal entity. It is described in Chapter 6 as part of the discussion concerning modelling principles and guidance.

MEIN

For MEIN, an entity is 'an object, concrete or abstract, that exists and is distinguishable; it can be a person, or a company or a distinction' (MEIN II 1991). Also, an entity is anything about which we want to store information.

MEIN classifies an entity as regular, weak or associative. A regular entity is one whose instances can be identified by themselves. That is, it has an *identifier* (see below) of its own.

The graphical representation of a regular entity is a rectangular box with its name written inside, as shown in Figure 2.2.

A weak entity is one whose occurrences are identified by being associated with one or more entities. The identifier (see below) of a weak entity is usually formed by its own identifier as well as the identifier of the related entity(s). For example, a section within an Aquaduct department requires the department name to identify it, as well as its own name, as this is not unique.

The graphical representation of a weak entity is a rectangular box with a double line and the name of the entity written inside, as in Figure 2.3.

MEIN also defines an associative entity which will be discussed in the chapter describing aggregation.

MERISE

For MERISE, 'an entity is a concept which is useful to the needs of the management of the firm' (Quang and Chartier-Kastler 1991). Alternatively, 'an entity is an abstract or concrete object in the universe of discourse' (Tardieu *et al.* 1983).

Figure 2.2   Regular entity employee (MEIN).

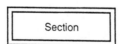

Figure 2.3   Weak entity section (MEIN).

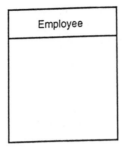

Figure 2.4   Entity employee (MERISE).

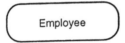

Figure 2.5   Entity employee (SSADM).

An entity is graphically represented by a rectangle containing a line, above which is the entity name, shown in Figure 2.4. The use of the empty part of the box under the name is discussed in the Attribute section below.

SSADM

For SSADM, 'an entity is an object or concept, either concrete or abstract, which is of importance to the area of business being investigated' (SSADM 1990). A link entity is described which is similar to the IE intersection entity and is discussed in Chapter 6.

An entity is graphically represented by a soft box with its name written inside and an example is shown in Figure 2.5.

ATTRIBUTE

Definitions

Attribute

An *attribute value* represents a descriptor or property of an entity instance, such as the age '45' or the name 'Smith' of a particular person. An *attribute type* represents a set or class of entity descriptors that describe the same entity type.

Examples of common attribute types are name, age, address and social security number, which might be typical descriptors of an entity type person.

Attributes describe entities in more detail.

As for entity and entity type, we follow normal practice and use the term attribute to refer to an attribute type.

Identifier

An *identifier* is, in its simplest form, an attribute, each value of which uniquely identifies an instance of an entity. For example, each value of the social security number attribute will uniquely identify an instance of the entity person.

The identifier is important as its values are employed by users to refer to and hence to retrieve and update entity instances, and by developers, in the design phases of systems development, to decide upon the data representation of entities.

An identifier may be simple or composite. If it is simple, it is typically a single attribute. A composite identifier may be made up of two or more attributes or a mixture of attributes and entities.

Attribute relationship constraints

These restrict the allowable combinations of an entity and an attribute, and there are two basic types of constraint, attribute relationship cardinality and optionality.

Attribute relationship cardinality
This defines the number of values of an attribute that may be associated with one instance of a related entity. It may also define the number of instances of the entity that may be associated with one value of the related attribute. There are four common types of cardinality combination, one:one, one:many, many:one and many:many, where the meaning of *many* is one, or more than one, value or instance.

Attribute relationship optionality
This defines whether or not all the instances of an entity must be associated with values of an attribute, and whether or not all the values of an attribute must be associated with instances of an entity. If they must be associated, this is termed *mandatory*, but if they only may be associated, this is termed *optional*.

It should be noted that attribute relationship cardinality and optionality define specific aspects of an attribute relationship at any instant in its existence in the organisation. These aspects may differ when the relationship is viewed over a period of time. For example, although employees may have only one address at any instant, an employee may move to many different addresses over a period of time.

IE

In IE an attribute is termed a *data item*. 'A data item is one which contains a single piece of information (attribute value) about an entity instance and it cannot be broken into parts that have meaning of their own'.

```
┌──────────────────┐
│                  │  card number, name,
│    Employee      │  address, telephone
│                  │  number
└──────────────────┘
```

Figure 2.6 Entity employee with attributes, showing the attribute card number as the identifier (IE).

Cardinality – the 'crow's foot' symbol represents *many* while the short line represents *one*. There may be many values of the attribute name but only one value of the attribute address associated to the entity.

Optionality – the small circle represents an optional relationship while its absence represents a mandatory relationship. The attribute name is optional but the attribute address is mandatory.

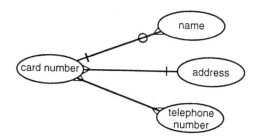

Figure 2.7 Bubble chart showing attributes of entity employee with attribute relationship constraints. The card number attribute is the identifier, representing the entity employee (IE).

For IE, identifiers are termed *primary keys*, while *non-key attributes* are those which do not uniquely identify an entity but are ordinary attributes of that entity.

Primary keys and some non-key attributes may be represented on the graphical model by writing them next to their related entity. The identifier is first in the list and is underlined (Martin and McClure 1985). An example of the graphical representation of attributes is shown in Figure 2.6.

IE allows all four cardinality types, so that an entity instance can have either one or many attribute values, and vice versa. In addition, attribute relationships may be specified as mandatory or optional. However, this can be defined only for the one:one or one:many cardinality types, specified from the entity direction.

These constraints are not shown on the diagram, but are specified separately. IE can do this graphically using a diagram termed the bubble chart, and an example for the employee entity and its attributes is shown in Figure 2.7, where attributes are shown in bubbles and the relationships between the card number identifier, representing the entity employee, and the other attributes are shown graphically by an edge connecting the bubbles.

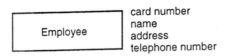

Figure 2.8 Entity employee with attributes (MEIN).

MEIN

An attribute in MEIN is defined as 'a basic and indivisible unit of information used to distinguish an entity' (MEIN II 1991). When an attribute is also an identifier it is termed a primary key.

An attribute of an entity may take a value from a set of possible values termed a *domain*. In addition, an attribute can be simple or composite. A composite attribute is made up of several attributes, for example the address attribute might be composed of the attributes house or apartment, street and postcode.

Attributes are documented separately with only the most important shown next to the entity to which they belong. Figure 2.8 shows an example of attributes for an entity.

MEIN does not provide a way to distinguish the identifier from other attributes. In addition, there is no difference between the graphical representation of a composite and a simple attribute. MEIN does not define attribute relationship cardinality or optionality.

MERISE

In MERISE, an attribute (also termed property) 'is an elementary data item which characterises an entity' (Quang and Chartier-Kastler 1991). A similar definition is 'an attribute is the representation of a property of an entity or the property of an association between entities' (Tardieu *et al*. 1983).

Only the most important properties are shown on the diagram. Their names can be written in the empty part of the box that represents the entity, as in Figure 2.9.

In Figure 2.9, the identifier can be first in the list of properties, or we can indicate which of the properties are identifiers by writing their names in a different style (Quang and Chartier-Kastler 1991) or by underlining the relevant property (Planche 1992).

As for MEIN, attribute relationship cardinality and optionality are not defined.

SSADM

For SSADM, 'an attribute is a characteristic of an entity, that is, any detail that serves to describe, qualify, identify, classify, quantify, or express the state of an entity' (SSADM 1990).

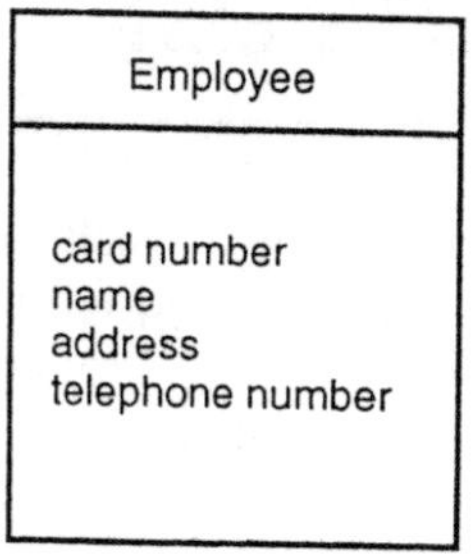

Employee
card number
name
address
telephone number

Figure 2.9 Entity employee with attributes, showing the attribute card number as the identifier (MERISE).

For SSADM, an attribute describes one entity only. Identifiers are not graphically distinguished from non-identifying attributes. When an entity has only a few attributes, they can be shown on the graphical model by writing them next to the entity to which they belong. An example is shown in Figure 2.10.

SSADM allows only one:one and many:one (from the entity direction) cardinality types, restricting an entity instance to have only one attribute value. Both mandatory and optional specification is available for attribute relationship optionality, but restricted to the entity only.

address
telephone number
Employee
card number
name

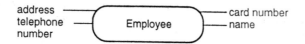

Figure 2.10 Entity employee with attributes (SSADM).

ENTITY–ATTRIBUTE LIST

Table 2.1 shows an entity–attribute list which describes attributes, their related entities and relevant constraints. As stated earlier, there is no standard for this description so we use the format of Table 2.1 for all the methods. Three entities and their attributes are detailed here, which illustrate all the points made above concerning attributes.

1. *Identifier*. The identifier is shown in Table 2.1 by underlining the relevant attribute or attributes. The section entity has a composite identifier, shown by the '/' separating the relevant attributes, as both department name and section name attributes are required to identify section. This is because section names are not unique over different departments.

2. *Composite attribute*. An address is shown as being composite, and is made up of a house or apartment, street and postcode.

3. *Attribute relationship constraints*. These are shown in the entity–attribute direction.

Table 2.1 Entity–attribute list

Entity	Attribute	Attribute relationship constraints
Department	department name	one:one; mandatory
Employee	card number	one:one; mandatory
	name	one:many; optional
	address (house/apt, street, postcode)	many:one; optional
	telephone number	many:many; optional
Section	department name/section name	one:one; mandatory

SUMMARY

Entity and attribute

Entity and attribute are defined by all the methods employing similar terms and the meaning is the same. Table 2.2 summarises the method correspondences for the entity and attribute concepts. MEIN is the only method to define the weak entity.

The methods also agree on their definitions of the identifier concept. Table 2.3 shows methods that have composite attributes and identifiers. Where * is shown, this type of attribute is shown in the graphical model.

Table 2.2 Entity and attribute

	Method			
Concept	IE	MERISE	MEIN	SSADM
Entity	yes	yes	yes	yes
Attribute	yes	yes	yes	yes

Table 2.3 Identifier and composite attribute

	Attributes	
Methods	Identifier	Composite
IE	yes*	–
MEIN	yes	yes
MERISE	yes*	–
SSADM	yes	–

Attribute relationship constraints

Differences

There are important differences concerning the concept of attribute relationship constraints, and Table 2.4 shows those that are allowed by the methods.

- *Attribute relationship cardinality.* IE allows all four cardinality types while SSADM allows only two types.

- *Attribute relationship optionality.* IE allows this, but only from the entity direction and when the attribute relationship cardinality is one:one or one:many. SSADM allows this for any cardinality but only from the entity direction.

- *MEIN and MERISE.* They do not define attribute relationship cardinality or optionality.

The last, surface, difference relates to the way in which attributes are graphically represented in the model. Table 2.5 shows how the methods represent entities and attributes in their graphical models.

Table 2.4 Attribute relationship cardinality and optionality

	Attribute relationship	
Method	Cardinality	Optionality
IE	one:one, one:many, many:one, many:many	mandatory/optional (in one:one and one:many only)
MEIN	–	–
MERISE	–	–
SSADM	one:one, many:one	mandatory/optional

Table 2.5 Graphical representation of entity and attributes (including identifiers)

Method	Entity with attributes

IE — Employee — card number, name / address / telephone number

MEIN — Employee — card number / name / address / telephone number — Section — weak entity

MERISE — Employee — card number / name / address / telephone number

SSADM — address, telephone number — Employee — card number, name

CONCLUSIONS

Reference framework concepts

- *Entity, attribute and identifier.* All methods provide these.

- *Attribute relationship constraints.* No method provides these fully.

Method scope

IE and SSADM have wider scope than MEIN and MERISE as they provide attribute relationship constraints (although with limitations). IE and SSADM can thus specify more detail concerning entity–attribute relationships than MEIN and MERISE.

Chapter 3

RELATIONSHIP

In this chapter, we discuss the reference framework concepts of binary relationship, relationship attribute, cardinality constraint and participation constraint.

We shall also briefly introduce the concept of *n*-ary relationship but the discussion will focus on binary relationships.

RELATIONSHIP

Definitions

Relationship

A *relationship* represents a meaningful association between entity types in an organisation. The entity types can be different or they can be the same.

The number of entity types participating in a relationship defines its degree. A *binary relationship* is where the number of participating entity types is equal to two, and an *n-ary relationship* is where the number of participating entity types is more than two.

A relationship has a relationship name, which may need to be unique, as more than one relationship may exist between the same entity types.

To define the concept of relationship more precisely:

> A relationship type represents a meaningful association between entity types in an organisation.

> A relationship instance represents a meaningful association between instances of entity types in an organisation.

To simplify terminology we use the term relationship to refer to a relationship type.

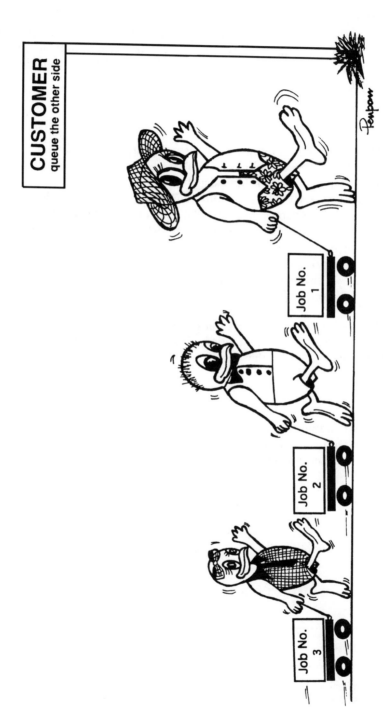

Instances of an entity may have relationships with instances of another entity.

Relationship attribute

A *relationship attribute* is an attribute which is associated with a relationship. For example, if an employee has a 'works-for' relationship with a company the date on which that relationship commenced may be recorded. This is modelled by the relationship attribute.

IE

In IE a relationship is also known as an 'association'. For IE, an association is 'a meaningful link between two objects' (Martin 1990). Also, the term association is used to indicate that 'a relationship exists between two entities different or of the same type' (Finkelstein 1989). In IE only binary associations are allowed.

IE employs the term 'label' (Martin 1990) instead of relationship name, and two different labels are used to express each of the directions of the relationship, viewed from each of the two entities.

The graphical representation of a relationship is a line connecting the two related entities. Figure 3.1 shows an example of a relationship linking pairs of entity instances of the same type, which is termed recursive. Here, only one label is needed.

Figure 3.2 represents a binary relationship linking two different entities, with two different labels to express each direction of the relationship. The labels are written next to the entities to which they apply.

MEIN

For MEIN a relationship, also known as an association, is 'a correspondence between two or more entities, which can be different or of the same type' (MEIN II 1991). *N*-ary relationships may thus exist in MEIN.

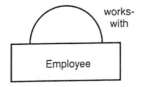

Figure 3.1 *Recursive relationship works-with. Employee works-with employee (IE).*

Figure 3.2 *Binary relationship between customer and customer account. The two different labels 'holds' and 'belongs to' are used to specify each direction of the relationship (IE).*

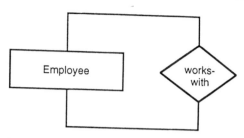

Figure 3.3 Recursive relationship works-with. Employee works-with employee (MEIN).

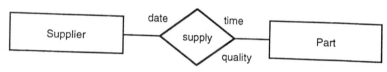

Figure 3.4 Binary relationship supply between supplier and part. Supply has attributes date, time and quality (MEIN).

A further characteristic of MEIN is that a relationship may have attributes. MEIN uses only one name for a relationship. The graphical representation of a relationship is a diamond shaped box containing its name, linked to the related entities by means of lines. An example of a recursive relationship may be seen in Figure 3.3.

A binary relationship between two different entities is shown in Figure 3.4, which also shows attributes of the relationship, which are written by the relationship symbol.

Figure 3.5 shows an example of an *n*-ary relationship where different entities participate in a three-way (ternary) relationship. The meaning of this relationship is that a customer has complained about a job order to a department. The complaint might be due, for example, to poor workmanship or faulty parts.

MERISE

For MERISE, a relationship is 'a semantic link between several entities independent of any processing' (Quang and Chartier-Kastler 1991) or 'a relationship is a perceived association between entities' (Rochfeld 1987).

For MERISE, binary and also *n*-ary relationships may be specified. MERISE uses the term dimension rather than degree to refer to the number of entities participating in a relationship (Tardieu *et al.* 1983).

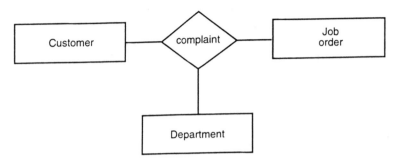

Figure 3.5 *N*-ary relationship complaint between the participating entities *department, job order* and *customer* (MEIN).

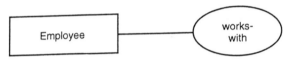

Figure 3.6 Reflexive relationship works-with. Employee works-with employee (MERISE).

Figure 3.7 Binary relationship *supply* between *supplier* and *part*. Supply has attributes *date, time* and *quality* (MERISE).

In MERISE a relationship uses only one name and it may have attributes. The graphical representation of a relationship is an ellipse with the name inside, linked to the related entities by means of lines.

Figures 3.6 and 3.7 represent different cases of binary relationships. In the first, the recursive relationship (termed *reflexive* in MERISE) links entity instances of the same type. In the second, the relationship links two different entities and possesses three attributes.

MERISE models the *n*-ary relationship described for MEIN as shown in Figure 3.8.

SSADM

In SSADM, only binary relationships are allowed and the term *relationship link phrase* is used instead of relationship name. The graphical representation of a

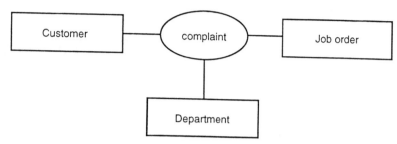

Figure 3.8 *N-ary relationship complaint between the participating entities department, job order and customer (MERISE).*

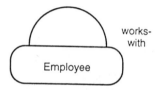

Figure 3.9 *Recursive relationship works-with. Employee works-with employee (SSADM).*

Figure 3.10 *Binary relationship between entities customer and customer account (SSADM).*

relationship is a line connecting the two related entities, and the names of the relationship link phrases are written next to the relevant entities. SSADM does not allow relationship attributes.

The recursive relationship, also known as involuted, is shown in Figure 3.9, and is termed 'pig's ear' because of its shape. Figure 3.10 shows an example where two different entities participate in a relationship.

CARDINALITY CONSTRAINT

Definition

The cardinality constraint is concerned with the number of instances of an entity which may be related to instances of the other entity in a relationship, and we may define the constraint more precisely as follows:

Instances of an entity may be related to different numbers of instances of another entity.

> The cardinality constraint of an entity A in a relationship R(AB) defines the number of instances of entity B which may be related to one instance of entity A.

We will use the shorter term cardinality rather than the term cardinality constraint. The most common cardinality values are *one* or *many* where the meaning of *many* is one, or more than one instance, and the cardinality constraint must be true at any time in the life of the entity.

If we combine the common cardinalities of the two entities in a binary relationship there are four possible values, referred to as the *cardinality ratio*. The four values are: one to one (1:1), one to many (1:N or 1:M), many to one (N:1 or M:1) and many to many (M:N).

IE

For IE the term cardinality refers to 'how many of one entity is associated with how many of another entity' (Martin 1990).

Figure 3.11 1:*N/N*:1 cardinality. A customer is associated with many customer accounts and a customer account is associated with one customer (IE).

Figure 3.12 1:1 cardinality. An advertising campaign is associated with one project and a project is associated with one advertising campaign (IE).

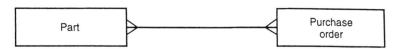

Figure 3.13 *M:N* cardinality. A purchase order is associated with many parts and a part is associated with many purchase orders (IE).

The cardinality constraint is specified using the *maximum cardinality indicator* in IE, which can take the values 1 or *N*, where *N* means many.

Maximum cardinality indicator = *N*. Where an instance of entity A may be related to many instances of entity B, the maximum cardinality indicator value for A is *N*. This is represented graphically by a 'crow's foot' placed nearest entity B across the line representing R(AB). Figure 3.11 shows this situation, where an instance of customer may be related to many instances of customer account. This is a 1:*N* cardinality ratio, from the customer direction.

Maximum cardinality indicator = *1*. Where an instance of entity A may be related to only one instance of entity B, the maximum cardinality indicator value for A is 1. This is represented graphically by a short line at right angles placed nearest entity B across the line representing R(AB). Figure 3.11 also shows this situation, where an instance of customer account (entity A) may be related to only one instance of customer (entity B). This is an example of an *N*:1 cardinality ratio, from the customer account direction.

We may note that an *N*:1 cardinality ratio is the inverse of a 1:*N* ratio.

IE thus employs what is termed a lookacross style (Ferg 1991) of cardinality, such that the cardinality of an entity A in a relationship R(AB) defines the number of instances of entity B that an instance of entity A sees when it 'looks across' the relationship R. Examples of 1:1 and *M:N* cardinality ratios are shown in Figures 3.12 and 3.13.

MEIN

In MEIN, the term *association degree* corresponds to the cardinality constraint, concerning the participation in the association of each of the relevant entities (MEIN II 1991).

Cardinality in MEIN is expressed using the concept of cardinality ratio discussed in the previous section. MEIN also adopts the lookacross style of relationship cardinality.

One to many (1:N). A one to many (1:N) cardinality ratio in a relationship R(AB), expressed in the A→B direction, is where an instance of entity A can be related to many instances of entity B, and an instance of entity B can be related to only one instance of entity A.

Figure 3.14 shows an example of the graphical representation of the 1:N cardinality ratio, where the character '1' next to an entity indicates that an instance of the other entity may be related to only one instance of this entity. The character M or N indicates that an instance of the other entity may be related to many instances of this entity.

One to one (1:1). A one to one (1:1) cardinality ratio in a relationship R(AB) is where an instance of entity A can be related to only one instance of entity B, and an instance of entity B can be related to only one instance of entity A.

To graphically represent a one to one cardinality ratio, the character '1' is placed next to both entities as shown in Figure 3.15.

Many to many (M:N). A many to many (M:N) cardinality ratio in a relationship R(AB) is where one instance of entity A can be related to many instances of entity B, and one instance of entity B can be related to many instances of entity A. Such an example is shown in Figure 3.16.

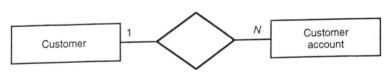

Figure 3.14　1:N cardinality. A customer is associated with many customer accounts and a customer account is associated with one customer (MEIN).

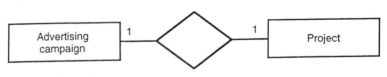

Figure 3.15　1:1 cardinality. An advertising campaign is associated with one project and a project is associated with one advertising campaign (MEIN).

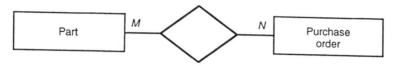

Figure 3.16 *M:N* cardinality. A purchase order is associated with many parts and a part is associated with many purchase orders (MEIN).

MERISE

The concept of cardinality in MERISE is similar in one respect to that of IE as it is concerned with the specification of a minimum and maximum number of instances. However, the similarity ends there as it is the number of instances of a *relationship* in which instances of an entity may participate that is specified. This is also termed 'connectivity' (Planche 1992).

The cardinality style in MERISE is therefore different and is termed participation style (Ferg 1991), as an entity instance is viewed as being linked to a relationship instance, instead of being related to an instance of another entity.

But as MERISE references state explicitly that a MERISE relationship instance can be linked to not more than one instance of each of the related entities (Collongues *et al.* 1989; Rochfeld 1987), the participation style is conceptually equivalent to the lookacross style.

MERISE provides the minimum (x) and maximum (y) cardinality parameters, specified together as (*x,y*). However, it is only the maximum cardinality parameter that expresses the meaning of the cardinality constraint, so we shall not discuss the *x* parameter in this section. The *maximum cardinality* parameter may take the value 1 or *N*, where *N* means many.

Maximum cardinality = *1*. The maximum cardinality of an entity A in a relationship R(AB) is 1 where an instance of entity A may participate in a maximum of one instance of the relationship R. To graphically represent this, we write the expression (*x*,1) by entity A.

Maximum cardinality = *N*. The maximum cardinality of an entity A in a relationship R(AB) is many where an instance of entity A may participate in many instances of the relationship *R*. To graphically represent this, we write the expression (*x,N*) by entity A.

Figure 3.17 shows an example of these two situations, where an instance of customer account may participate in only one instance of the relationship with customer, and an instance of customer may participate in many instances of the relationship with customer account. The cardinality ratio of the relationship is thus equivalent to 1:*N*, from the customer direction.

The major difference between the lookacross and the participation styles is therefore only one of surface, graphical representation. The lookacross style represents the cardinality of, for example, entity A next to entity B, while the participation style represents the cardinality of entity A next to entity A.

Figure 3.17 1:N/N:1 cardinality. A customer is associated with many customer accounts and a customer account is associated with one customer (MERISE).

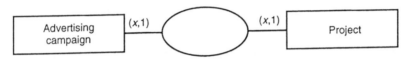

Figure 3.18 1:1 cardinality. An advertising campaign is associated with one project and a project is associated with one advertising campaign (MERISE).

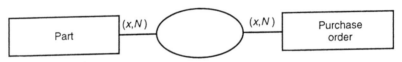

Figure 3.19 M:N cardinality. A purchase order is associated with many parts and a part is associated with many purchase orders (MERISE).

A relationship linking two entities, both with cardinality $(x,1)$, is equivalent to a one to one (1:1) cardinality ratio, as shown in Figure 3.18. If two entities with cardinality (x,N) participate in a relationship, as seen in Figure 3.19, this is equivalent to a many to many ($M:N$) cardinality ratio.

SSADM

In SSADM, the concept of cardinality constraint is known as *relationship degree*, and refers to the number of instances of an entity to which an instance of another entity may be related. The cardinality style that SSADM adopts is the lookacross style (Ferg 1991). The four common types of relationship cardinality ratio are defined.

One to many. To graphically represent a one to many (1:N) cardinality ratio, a 'crow's foot' symbol placed on the relationship line by an entity indicates that an instance of the other entity may be related to many instances of this entity. A plain

Figure 3.20 1:*N*/*N*:1 cardinality. A customer is associated with many customer accounts and a customer account is associated with one customer (SSADM).

Figure 3.21 1:1 cardinality. An advertising campaign is associated with one project and a project is associated with one advertising campaign (SSADM).

Figure 3.22 *M*:*N* cardinality. A purchase order is associated with many parts and a part is associated with many purchase orders (SSADM).

Figure 3.23 Fixed degree. A customer is associated with exactly two salesmen (SSADM).

line by an entity indicates that an instance of the other entity may be related to only one instance of this entity. An example is shown in Figure 3.20.

One to one. SSADM graphically represents the one to one (1:1) cardinality ratio with a plain line which joins the related entities, as shown in Figure 3.21.

Many to many. The many to many (*M*:*N*) cardinality ratio is graphically represented by a line which joins entity A to entity B with a 'crow's foot' at both ends, as shown in Figure 3.22.

Fixed degree. Sometimes the number of instances of an entity that may be related to an instance of another entity is fixed. To represent fixed degree graphically, the number of instances of entity B that can be related to an instance of entity A is written next to entity B. An example of this is shown in Figure 3.23.

PARTICIPATION CONSTRAINT

Definition

The *participation constraint* of an entity specifies whether or not all the instances of the entity must participate in a relationship with instances of the other entity.

There are two types of participation constraint, *total* and *partial*, which we define considering the participation of the instances of an entity A in a relationship R(AB).

Total participation

Where all instances of entity A must participate in the relationship with instances of entity B, the participation of A in the relationship R(AB) is termed total.

In this situation, often termed *mandatory* participation, an instance of entity A cannot exist without being related to entity B.

Partial participation

Where some, not necessarily all, instances of entity A may participate in the relationship with instances of entity B, the participation of A in the relationship R(AB) is termed partial.

In this situation, often termed *optional* participation, an instance of entity A can exist without being related to entity B.

The participation constraint must be true at any time in the life of the entity.

IE

In IE, the concept of participation constraint is specified by the *minimum cardinality indicator* for an entity in a relationship, which may take only two values, 0 or 1. When the value is 0, it is equivalent to the optional participation of the entity in the relationship. When the value is 1, it is equivalent to the mandatory participation of the entity in the relationship.

A third concept is also defined as 'optional tending to mandatory' or 'transitional association' (Finkelstein 1989). This concept allows the participation of an entity in a relationship to be optional for a given time, and after that to assume a mandatory participation. The style for expressing the participation constraint in IE is the lookacross style (Ferg 1991).

Instances of an entity may or may not participate in a relationship with instances of another entity.

Figure 3.24 *A job order may be associated with a project, but a project must be associated with a job order (IE).*

Figure 3.25 *A supplier may be recorded initially without a supplier account, but should be associated with one later (early version of IE).*

To graphically represent the mandatory participation of an entity A in the relationship R(AB), a short line at right angles crossing the relationship line is placed next to entity B, and to represent the optional participation of entity A, a small circle crossing the relationship line is placed next to entity B. Figure 3.24 shows an example.

To represent an optional tending to mandatory participation for entity A, the short line and the small circle crossing the association line are placed next to entity B. Figure 3.25 shows an example.

MEIN

MEIN does not provide the participation constraint.

MERISE

In the earlier cardinality constraint section of this chapter dealing with MERISE, the cardinality parameters (x,y) for an entity in a relationship were mentioned and we emphasised the maximum cardinality parameter (y) in that discussion.

We now develop our description of the minimum cardinality parameter as it corresponds to the concept of participation constraint, specifying the minimum number of instances of a relationship to which each instance of an entity must be linked.

The minimum cardinality for an entity may take one of two values, 0 or 1. If the value is 0, it is equivalent to the optional participation of the entity in the relationship, and if the value is 1, it is equivalent to the mandatory participation of

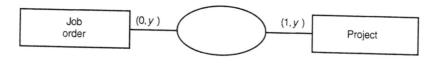

Figure 3.26 A job order may be associated with a project, but a project must be associated with a job order (MERISE).

the entity in the relationship. The style for expressing the participation constraint in MERISE is the participation style (Ferg 1991).

To represent graphically the mandatory participation of an entity A in the relationship R(AB), the expression (1,y) is written next to entity A; while for optional participation of entity A, the expression (0,y) is written next to entity A. An example is shown in Figure 3.26.

Some authors (Rochfeld 1987; Tardieu *et al.* 1983) use the term total and partial relationship to refer to the participation constraint on both sides of a relationship considered as a whole.

SSADM

SSADM uses the terms *mandatory* and *optional* to describe the two types of participation constraint. The style for expressing the participation constraint in SSADM is the participation style.

To graphically represent mandatory participation, SSADM uses a solid relationship line next to the mandatory entity, and to represent optional participation, SSADM uses a dashed line, as in Figure 3.27.

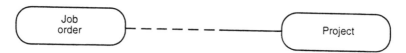

Figure 3.27 A job order may be associated with a project, but a project must be associated with a job order (SSADM).

SUMMARY

Binary relationship and cardinality constraint

All methods provide these concepts although they all use different terms for cardinality constraint.

Participation constraint

MEIN does not provide this concept. All other methods provide this although they all use different terms.

Relationship attribute

MEIN and MERISE provide this but IE and SSADM do not. However, relationships with attributes may be modelled in IE and SSADM using intersection or link entities. An example is discussed in Chapter 6.

Table 3.1 shows the correspondences between the reference framework and method concepts as well as the differences in terminology.

Table 3.1 Relationship concepts

| Concept | Methods | | | |
	IE	MEIN	MERISE	SSADM
Binary relationship	yes	yes	yes	yes
Term to refer to a relationship among same entity types	recursive	recursive	reflexive	pig's ear
Relationship name	label (two labels allowed)	relationship name (only one)	relationship name (only one)	relationship link phrase (two names allowed)
Relationship with attribute	–	yes	yes	–
Relationship constraint definition	cardinality and participation	cardinality	cardinality and participation	cardinality and participation
Cardinality style	lookacross	lookacross	participation	lookacross
Participation	mandatory and optional	–	mandatory and optional	mandatory and optional
Participation style	lookacross	–	participation	participation

Minor differences

MEIN and MERISE permit only one name for a relationship, whereas IE and SSADM allow one name for each direction of the relationship.

Tables 3.2 to 3.4 show the different, surface graphical representations of different concepts.

Table 3.2 *Graphical representation of a relationship, including relationships with attributes*

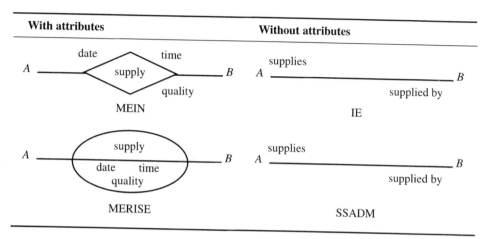

With attributes	Without attributes

Table 3.3 *Cardinality types*

Method	Graphical representation of relationship cardinality		
	one to one (1:1)	one to many (1:N)	many to many (M:N)
IE			
MEIN	1 ... 1	1 ... N	M ... N
MERISE	(x,1) ... (x,1)	(x, N) ... (x, 1)	(x, N) ... (x, N)
SSADM			2 (fixed degree)

CONCLUSIONS

The methods differ for the relationship concepts discussed in this chapter.

Reference framework concepts

- *Binary relationship and cardinality constraint.* All methods provide these.
- *Participation constraint.* MEIN does not provide this.
- *Relationship attribute.* IE and SSADM do not provide this.

Table 3.4 Graphical representation of participation constraint

Method	Relationship participation	
	$A \rightarrow B$ mandatory	$B \rightarrow A$ optional
IE	A ──○───────────── ├─ B	
MEIN	not defined	
MERISE	A ──(1,y)───────⬭──── (0,y) B	
SSADM	A ─────────── ─ ─ ─ ─ ─ B	

Method scope

- MEIN does not support the concept of participation constraint.
- MEIN and MERISE permit only one name for a relationship. This may reduce the meaning captured on the diagram.

Graphical representations

On the surface, graphical representations make the methods appear very different but the concepts represented are equivalent.

Chapter 4

MULTIPLE RELATIONSHIP

In Chapter 3 we explained the meaning of relationship in the methods. We based the discussion on the capability of the methods for modelling relationships between two entities only, using the binary relationship concept.

However, it is often the case in organisations that there are relationships involving more than two entities, and we term such a relationship a *multiple relationship*. We distinguish between the multiple relationship in the organisation and the *n-ary relationship* reference framework concept, and we describe the corresponding concept used by the methods to model different types of multiple relationships.

DEFINITION

The definition of a multiple relationship is as follows:

> A multiple relationship is a relationship between more than two entities, which is regarded in an application as a unit or combination that cannot be split for semantic reasons.

We term the entities that are involved in such a combination *participating entities*. The general definition of the relationship concept given in Chapter 3 also applies to the *n*-ary relationship concept.

In this chapter we will discuss how the methods model multiple relationships. MEIN and MERISE provide a special concept for this, the *n*-ary relationship concept, while IE and SSADM only provide the binary relationship concept. We will also see how the methods cope with multiple relationships where different cardinality and participation constraints apply.

A multiple relationship concerns a relationship between two or more entities.

MULTIPLE RELATIONSHIP MODELLING USING THE *N*–ARY RELATIONSHIP CONCEPT

MEIN and MERISE

Our first example of a multiple relationship was briefly introduced in Chapter 3 and concerns three related entities, customer, job order and department, which we describe in more detail here.

The meaning of this relationship is that a customer may make a complaint concerning a job order to a department. The cardinality ratios between all pairs of entities are *M:N*, such that, for example, a customer may complain about many job orders, a department may be complained to by many customers, and vice versa.

The important point is that we want to be able to model the fact that there is a *combination* of the entities; for example, that a given customer has complained to a certain department concerning a certain job order. The *n*-ary relationship concept in MEIN and MERISE models the meaning of this combination of entities, and the relationship, complaint, is shown in Figure 4.1. Implicitly, a joint instance each of the participating entities uniquely identifies one instance of complaint.

In Figure 4.1, for MEIN, the characters *M*, *N* and *P* graphically represent the *M:N* cardinality ratios between entities. For MERISE, the *M:N* cardinality ratios

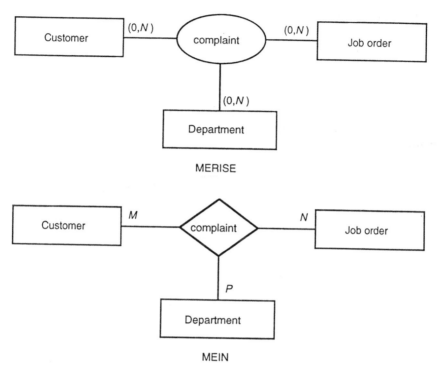

Figure 4.1 Multiple relationship complaint with participating entities customer, job order and department, using the *n*-ary relationship concept (MEIN and MERISE).

are represented by the maximum cardinality value of N for each entity, which specifies that an entity instance may participate in many instances of the relationship complaint, each instance of which is the combination of one instance each of the participating entities.

MULTIPLE RELATIONSHIP MODELLING USING THE BINARY RELATIONSHIP CONCEPT

IE and SSADM provide only the binary relationship concept for modelling relationships. To avoid problems in modelling multiple relationships with this concept it is necessary to create an 'abstract entity' and to relate this to the participating entities. We discuss this topic first. Then we describe the two basic approaches to modelling a multiple relationship using the binary relationship concept: the N-ary approach and the nested binary approach.

Binary relationship concept problems

Let us consider the multiple relationship above with the three participating entities customer, job order and department. Figure 4.2 shows how this relationship might be modelled by IE and SSADM, using the binary relationship concept with only the participating entities.

Let us consider the situation where two customers *C1* and *C2* complain about a job order *J1*; *C1* complains to department *D1* and *C2* complains to department *D2*. Our model needs to be able to record, for a given customer, which job order is complained about to which department.

Figure 4.3 represents the entity and relationship instances which are capable of being recorded by the model in Figure 4.2. There are two facts recorded:

1. The binary relationship between customer and job order in Figure 4.2 can record the fact that customers *C1* and *C2* complain about job order *J1*.

2. The binary relationship between job order and department in Figure 4.2 can record the fact that job order *J1* is related to departments *D1* and *D2*.

However, we cannot infer from these two facts whether it is department *D1* or *D2* that customer *C1* complains to concerning job order *J1*.

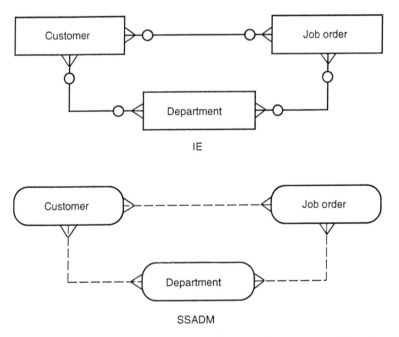

IE

SSADM

Figure 4.2 Binary relationships with participating entities customer, job order and department (IE and SSADM).

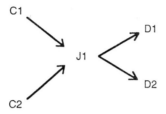

Figure 4.3 Job order J1 has two related customers and two departments, but does not record which customers are related to which departments.

The relationship between customer and department in Figure 4.2 cannot help as, for example, customer *C1* may have complained to department *D1* concerning another job order, *J3*.

In general, we cannot model a multiple relationship correctly by using binary relationships between only the participating entities. The information we wish to record concerns all participating entities considered as a unit, and it cannot be recorded as an aggregation of information contained in the binary relationships. As we said in the introduction to the chapter, the combination cannot be split.

N-ary approach to multiple relationship modelling

In the *N*-ary approach, a new, abstract entity which we name complaint is built from the entities customer, job order and department. Complaint is associated with the participating entities with binary relationships. The meaning of an instance of complaint is that one customer complains about one job order to one department.

The participation of the abstract entity in these relationships is mandatory, and its cardinality ratio with the participating entities is *N*:1. Figure 4.4 shows this. The required information is recorded as an instance of customer is associated with several instances of complaint, each instance of which is associated with one instance of job order and one instance of department.

The fact that a joint instance each of customer, job order and department uniquely identifies an instance of complaint is modelled in IE and SSADM by specifying, on the entity-attribute list, the identifier of complaint to be a combination of the identifiers of the participating entities.

Concept of combination entity

In the example above, there is a naturally occurring name, complaint, for the relationship with which users are familiar and which is required to be preserved in the model. We term this a *combination entity*, and it is a named, abstract object employed by the user to express the combination of the participating entities.

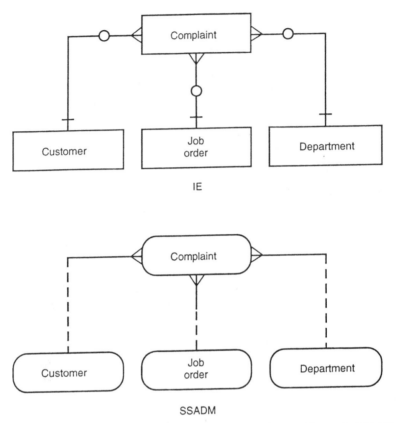

Figure 4.4 *Multiple relationship complaint with participating entities customer, job order and department, using the binary relationship concept (IE and SSADM).*

However, such an entity may not always be present in a multiple relationship, and the designer may have to invent a name for the abstract entity that is required to link the participating entities. For example, suppose the case study had an extra requirement to record which employees (E) worked for which customers (C) on which job orders (J), ECJ may be used as the name of the new abstract entity, which we may term a 'designer' entity.

In this case, the modelling is identical to that in IE and SSADM above, where the abstract entity name would be ECJ, as shown in Figure 4.5.

Nested binary approach to multiple relationship modelling

This approach groups together two entities and forms an abstract entity that is dependent on their combination. In this example, we choose customer and job

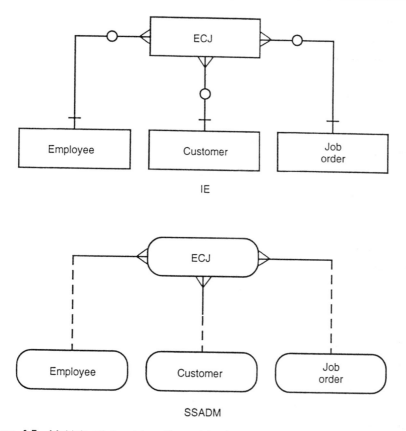

Figure 4.5 Multiple relationship with participating entities employee, customer, and job order, using the binary relationship concept and the 'designer' entity ECJ (IE and SSADM).

order, creating the abstract entity custjob, with the meaning of a unique combination of one customer complaining about one job order. This is then related to the third entity department using a binary relationship. The result of this approach is shown in Figure 4.6.

The participation of the abstract entity in these relationships is mandatory. It should also be noted that the cardinality ratio of the abstract entity in its relationship with the unnested entity department is $M:N$, in contrast to Figure 4.5.

Customer and job order are thus 'nested' to form an abstract, 'designer' entity that we term custjob. The identifier of custjob should be specified appropriately to indicate that its instances are uniquely identified by a joint instance each of customer and job order. The required information is recorded as an instance of department is associated with several instances of custjob, each instance of which is associated with one instance only of customer and job order.

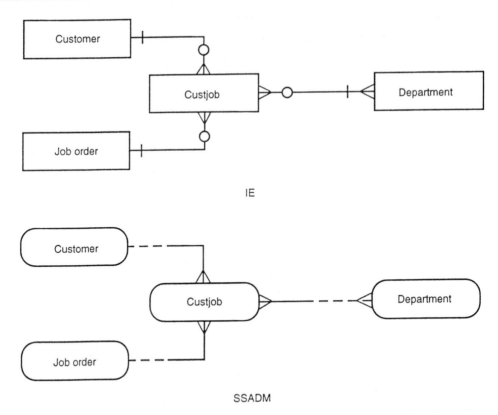

Figure 4.6 *Multiple relationship with participating entities customer, job order and department, using the binary relationship concept (IE and SSADM).*

Effectiveness of binary relationship concept

It should be noted that, as described above, none of the methods provides suitable graphical means for representing the identifiers of abstract entities, which diminishes the effectiveness of using this concept to model multiple relationships. For example, in Figure 4.6, suppose another entity project was associated with a binary relationship to custjob. How would we know from looking at the diagram whether or not it was a joint identifier of custjob?

MULTIPLE RELATIONSHIP CARDINALITY

Introduction

Only the simplest case so far has been used for the example of a multiple relationship, where the only cardinality constraints that applied were the many to many ($M:N$) cardinality ratios of the participating entities. How do the methods cope with modelling multiple relationships where the cardinalities are different?

In order to discuss this, we choose two examples, based on the same multiple relationship, which will display the scope and limitations of the n-ary relationship concept in the methods. We vary the cardinalities of the participating entities and then show the modelling of the resulting multiple relationship.

We consider the following two examples:

> **Example 1.** An instance of one entity may be related to one instance only of the other entities.

> **Example 2.** Two entities together determine a third entity.

We shall use the multiple relationship presentation, involving the entities manager, job order and customer, as our basic example. An instance of presentation represents the fact that a manager can make a presentation about the experience of a job order concerning a customer.

Presentation is thus a combination entity, as discussed above, whose name is to be preserved. One reason for this might be that this name distinguishes the relationship from other multiple relationships which may exist involving the same participating entities, such as 'complaints designate' or 'quality controller'.

Example 1

For the first example, we consider the situation where a manager can make a presentation about only one job order and one customer. In this case, there are two $N:1$ cardinality ratios (manager:job order, manager:customer), so not all cardinality ratios are $M:N$.

MEIN

In MEIN, it is not possible to model this situation using the n-ary relationship concept, as its lookacross style of cardinality means that, for a given cardinality value next to an entity, we cannot know which entity is 'looking across' to that entity. Instead, binary relationships must be used, as described for IE and SSADM below.

MERISE

As MERISE employs the participation style, it can model the relationship using the n-ary relationship concept, as shown in Figure 4.7.

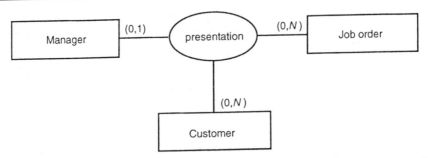

Figure 4.7 *Multiple relationship presentation using the n-ary relationship concept. A manager can make a presentation about only one job order concerning only one customer (MERISE).*

IE and SSADM

Binary relationships in any of the methods may be used to model this example, and Figure 4.8 shows how this may be done in SSADM and IE.

A manager instance is related to only one instance of the combination entity presentation, which in turn is related to only one instance of job order and one instance of customer. Thus an instance of presentation records the fact that one manager can make a presentation about one job order concerning one customer.

Note that we must use the combination entity in conjunction with the participating entities to model the situation correctly. If we omit the combination entity then we lose the name presentation. Such an omission may introduce errors, especially when we design transactions based on the entities and relationships. Such transactions may not, for example, insert instances of all four entities together, as required by the meaning of the relationship.

Example 2

For the second case, we consider the situation where two entities determine a third entity. We vary the cardinalities of the example so that a particular customer and job order uniquely determine the manager. That is, a presentation concerning the experience of a particular job order at a particular customer is always given by the same manager. In addition, the cardinality ratios of all the participating entities are *M:N*.

MEIN

This example can be modelled in MEIN, using the *n*-ary relationship concept, as in Figure 4.9, where the meaning of the cardinality value of 1 next to the manager

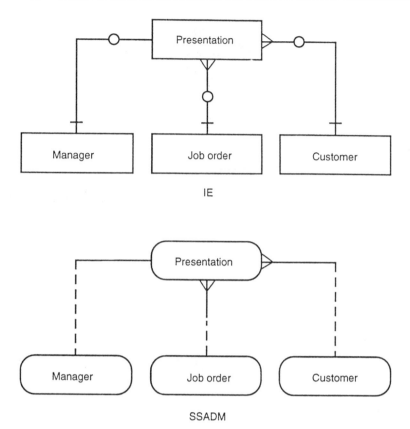

Figure 4.8 Multiple relationship presentation using the binary relationship concept. A manager can make a presentation about only one job order concerning only one customer (IE and SSADM).

entity is that a joint instance each of customer and job order uniquely determines a manager instance.

MERISE

As MERISE employs the participation style it cannot model this relationship using the *n*-ary relationship concept alone. However, we show in the next chapter that MERISE can use the functional integrity constraint to model this relationship.

IE and SSADM

Binary relationships in any of the methods may be used to model this example, and Figure 4.10 shows how this may be done in SSADM and IE, using the nested binary

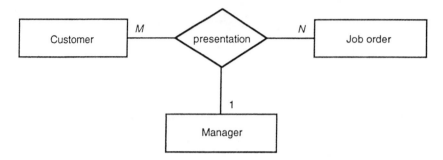

Figure 4.9 Multiple relationship presentation using the *n*-ary relationship concept. A customer and a job order uniquely determine a manager (MEIN).

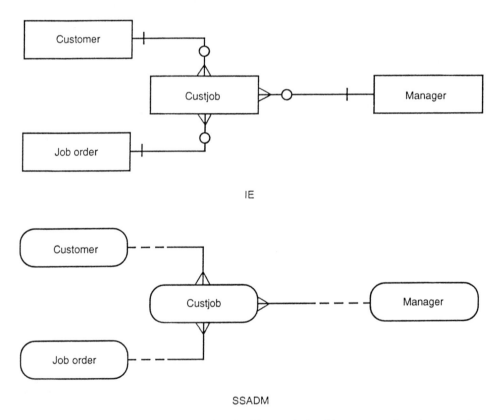

IE

SSADM

Figure 4.10 Multiple relationship using the binary relationship concept. A customer and a job order uniquely determine a manager (IE and SSADM).

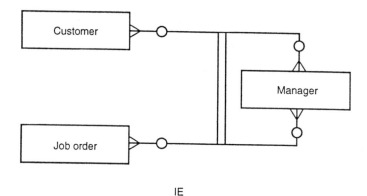

IE

Figure 4.11 *Extended associations in IE (early version). A customer and a job order relate to the same manager.*

approach, where an abstract entity custjob (also requiring an appropriate identifier to specify that a joint instance each of customer and job order uniquely identifies an instance of custjob) is defined to enforce the restriction on manager.

An early version of IE (Finkelstein 1989; Martin and Finkelstein 1981) may model this example using a type of association termed extended association. For this particular case, Figure 4.11 expresses the fact that the association or customer:manager and the association job order:manager both relate to the same manager.

MULTIPLE RELATIONSHIP PARTICIPATION

In this example we do not vary the cardinalities of the participating entities but instead vary a participation constraint. This is to highlight the assumption, made in the previous examples in this chapter, that the combination entity always has a mandatory relationship with all the participating entities.

We use the multiple relationship in Figure 4.4, concerning the relationship complaint, and we change a participation constraint, so that although a complaint usually consists of a customer, job order and department, the department is optional for some complaints.

This situation may occur where a customer may not complain about a job order to a specific department, and Aquaduct do not decide on the appropriate department until some time after the complaint is made.

MEIN and MERISE

This relationship cannot be modelled using the *n*-ary relationship concept in MEIN and MERISE. The implicit rule in this concept is that an instance of the relationship must be linked to one instance of each of the participating entities.

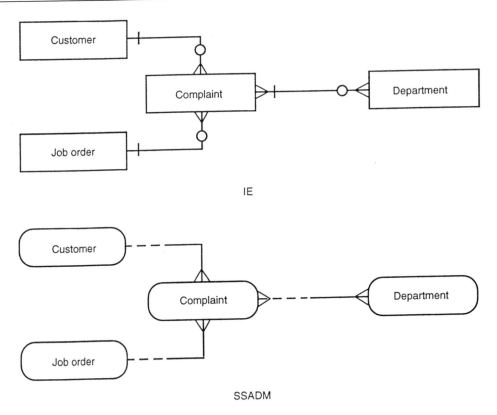

Figure 4.12 *Multiple relationship using the binary relationship concept. A complaint-related customer and a job order need not be associated with a department (IE and SSADM).*

IE and SSADM

The nested binary approach, using the binary relationship concept, can model this situation, and this is shown in Figure 4.12, where the combination entity complaint has an optional relationship with department.

SUMMARY

N-ary and binary relationship concepts

In the first section of this chapter, we discussed how MEIN and MERISE can model multiple relationships using the *n*-ary relationship concept. We then discussed how IE and SSADM provide only the binary relationship concept to

Table 4.1 Multiple relationship modelling

| | Method | | | | | |
| | MEIN | | MERISE | | IE | SSADM |
Situation	*n*-ary relationship concept	binary relationship concept	*n*-ary relationship concept	binary relationship concept	binary relationship concept	binary relationship concept
Unrestricted	yes	yes	yes	yes	yes	yes
Cardinality variation 1	no	yes	yes	yes	yes	yes
Cardinality variation 2	yes	yes	yes (needs extra constraint)	yes	yes	yes
Participation variation	no	yes	no	yes	yes	yes

model multiple relationships and we described the *N*-ary and nested binary approaches using this.

The *N*-ary approach uses an abstract entity to relate the participating entities in a multiple relationship using the binary relationship concept. The nested binary approach uses an abstract entity that relates the participating entities with the binary relationship concept, where two of the entities are nested together.

We then explored deviations from the 'straightforward' case by looking at variations in multiple relationships as they arise naturally in organisations. We discussed two cardinality variations and one participation variation, all of which gave some problems to one or more methods when using the *n*-ary relationship concept.

Table 4.1 shows the capabilities of the methods for modelling the different examples of multiple relationships we have described, including variations in cardinality and participation. The unrestricted case refers to the example in Figure 4.1 where there are no restrictions. Cardinality variations refer to the examples in which (1) cardinality ratios are other than *M:N*, and (2) two entities together determine a third entity. The participation variation refers to the example where an entity instance may exist without being related to an instance of the combination of participating entities.

Identifiers for binary relationship concept

It should be noted that the *N*-ary and nested binary approaches to modelling depend heavily upon the correct definition of identifiers for the abstract entities.

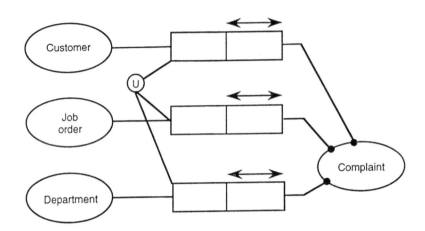

Figure 4.13 *Multiple relationship complaint using the binary relationship concept and illustrating the use of the uniqueness constraint (NIAM).*

None of the methods provides suitable graphical means for representing this, and their effectiveness is thus diminished.

NIAM (Nijssen and Halpin 1989) is an example of a method which does this graphically and more explicitly using the uniqueness constraint. An example of this is shown in Figure 4.13, where the uniqueness constraint (represented by the 'U') links those entities which form the composite identifier of the combination entity. The figure corresponds to the example in Figure 4.4.

Modelling guidance and quality criteria

The concepts discussed in this chapter have raised the issue of modelling choice, as a method may provide more than one concept to model a given situation. In these circumstances, modelling guidance is required, not only to choose the right concept to model the situation correctly, but also to choose between concepts on the basis of *quality criteria*, which are criteria that may be applied to help build an information model of high quality.

For example, the criterion of *naturalness* is that method concepts should correspond to concepts in the user's organisation, and this may be applied to choose the *n*-ary relationship rather than the binary relationship for modelling the unrestricted case of multiple relationships, on the basis that the *n*-ary relationship corresponds to the multiple relationship more directly than several binary relationships.

CONCLUSIONS

Reference framework concepts

- The n-ary relationship concept is present in only two of the methods, MERISE and MEIN.

- All methods provide the binary relationship concept, which can model all the multiple relationship variations presented.

  However, the binary relationship is deficient in its graphical representation as identifiers are not shown, which are crucial for multiple relationship modelling. This should be improved in the methods.

- The examples in this chapter have shown that modelling choice is unavoidable, with guidance being required, as the n-ary relationship concept in some methods cannot model certain types of multiple relationship.

Modelling guidance

- The n-ary relationship concept is a natural approach to modelling multiple relationships where cardinality and participation constraints are 'straightforward', as discussed above.

- Where multiple relationships are not 'straightforward', involving variations in the cardinality and participation constraints of participating entities, it may not be possible to model them in a given method using the n-ary relationship concept.

- The decision concerning which binary relationship approach to use may depend on the values of the participation constraint. If the entities must all be related together at the same time, either approach is appropriate. However, if the possibility exists for relating one entity at a later stage, the nested binary approach is the only choice.

- Tables 4.2 and 4.3 suggest the main advantages and disadvantages when using the binary or the n-ary relationship concepts for multiple relationship modelling.

Table 4.2 Advantages and disadvantages in modelling multiple relationships with the binary relationship concept

Advantages	Disadvantages
• Can model all multiple relationship examples discussed	• Choice of using nested or *n*-ary approach, therefore multiple relationship modelling not natural
	• Model may be overcomplex
	• Have to use an abstract entity
	• Identifier of abstract entity has no graphical representation

Table 4.3 Advantages and disadvantages in modelling multiple relationships with the *n*-ary relationship concept

Advantages	Disadvantages
• Multiple situation modelling is natural	• Some methods cannot model all cardinality and participation variations shown
• No need to create abstract entity	

Chapter 5

GENERALISATION, AGGREGATION AND RULE

This chapter discusses the reference framework concepts of generalisation, property inheritance, multiple inheritance, exclusion, exhaustion, aggregation and rule. These may be seen as 'higher-order' concepts as they are expressed in terms of combinations of more basic concepts such as entity, attribute and relationship.

GENERALISATION

Definitions

Generalisation abstraction

Generalisation is an abstraction process whereby a set of similar types is regarded as a higher-level, generic type (Smith and Smith 1977; Tsichritzis and Lochovsky 1982).

Generalisation is most commonly applied to entities. In this case, generalisation establishes the 'is-a' relationship between an entity and a more generic entity, so that an instance of the lower-level entity 'is-a' instance of the higher-level entity (but not vice versa).

We will use the terms (*entity*) *supertype* and *subtype* for the higher- and lower-level entities respectively. A set of subtypes together with their supertype and the 'is-a' relationships between them constitute a *generalisation hierarchy*.

Property inheritance

The principle of *property inheritance* is that a subtype possesses or 'inherits' the attributes and relationships (properties) associated with its supertype.

Inheritance is a useful concept in a generalisation hierarchy as attributes or relationships that are common to many subtypes are specified only once on the

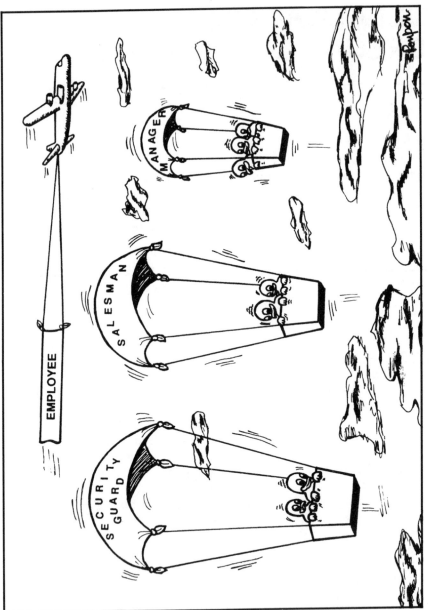

Entities may be subtypes of another entity.

supertype, and do not have to be repeated on subtypes that also possess those properties.

Multiple inheritance

Many generalisation hierarchies permit a subtype to have only one supertype. The situation where a subtype may have more than one supertype is termed *multiple inheritance*.

You should be careful to distinguish between the two types of inheritance, as property inheritance is often referred to simply as inheritance.

IE

IE defines an *entity subtype* as any subset of entity instances of a specific entity about which we want to record information that is special to that subtype (Martin 1990). Subtypes may exist in an entity hierarchy.

Subtypes are graphically represented as divisions of the entity box, where each division corresponds to a subtype, as shown in Figure 5.1.

This is only a small hierarchy chosen for the case study to illustrate the principle of generalisation. The figure shows that employee is a generic entity, and there are three main kinds of employee: security guard, salesperson and manager. Security guard and salesperson are also supertypes (as well as being subtypes of employee)

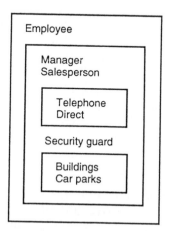

Figure 5.1 *Employee has manager, security guard and salesperson subtypes. Security guard has subtypes buildings and car parks and salesperson has subtypes telephone and direct (IE).*

Table 5.1 Entity–attribute list for employee subtypes

Entity	Attribute
Employee	<u>card number</u> name address (house/apartment, street, postcode) telephone number
Manager	parking place number (*inherits employee attributes*)

Salesperson
  telephone
  direct
	sales club number
	(*inherits employee attributes*)

Security guard
  buildings
  car parks
	(*inherits employee attributes*)

and they have two subtypes each, so that a security guard can be assigned to buildings or car parks, and a salesperson can be a telephone or a direct salesperson.

Subtypes may have attributes in addition to those of the supertype, and these are shown for the manager and salesperson subtypes in Table 5.1, which is an extract from the entity–attribute list in Chapter 6.

IE does not provide the property inheritance concept, so the attributes of employee would have to be duplicated on each of its subtypes in Table 5.1.

IE suggests that the values of one or more attributes of the supertype can be used to determine the subtype to which a specific entity instance belongs, and those attributes are termed *classifying attributes*. For example, the classifying attribute of the employee entity may be card number, the last three digits of which may be coded to indicate seniority and job description.

The classifying attribute of the salesperson supertype might be the sales club number attribute, such that the first digit is either a 'D' (for a direct salesperson) or 'T' (for a telephone salesperson). There is no standard form for showing such attribute values or their meaning.

MEIN

MEIN explains generalisation by defining entity supertype and subtype. An entity supertype is formed by one or more entity subtypes, and an entity subtype is one that inherits attributes from its supertype (MEIN II 1991).

Generalisation is graphically represented by connecting the entity supertype to its entity subtypes with a line, usually arranged hierarchically from the top of the diagram, as in Figure 5.2. MEIN does not graphically represent property inheritance on the model.

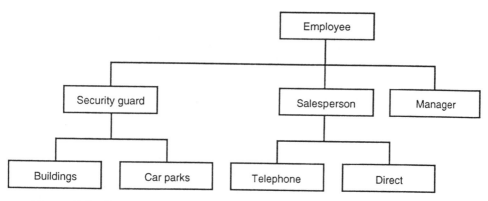

Figure 5.2 *Generalisation hierarchy showing supertype employee with manager, salesperson and security guard subtypes. Security guard has subtypes buildings and car parks and salesperson has subtypes telephone and direct (MEIN).*

MERISE

For MERISE, generalisation is the view of a type of entity object as a generic object, and a specialised entity type is one which descends from several generic types (Tardieu *et al*. 1983). Another definition is: 'generalizations of entities are super-entities and specializations are sub-entities' (Planche 1992).

MERISE represents generalisation with arrowed lines pointing from the entity subtype to the generic entity, as in Figure 5.3. To represent specialisation, arrows point from the generic entity towards the specialised entities, as in Figure 5.4. This representation is obviously ambiguous as the arrows may represent either generalisation or specialisation. Also, MERISE may use the relationship name 'is-a' to clearly identify a subtype–supertype hierarchy.

MERISE provides the property inheritance concept, where entity subtypes inherit all the properties of a generic entity, and inheritance can be graphically represented. Figure 5.5 shows an example of inheritance where employee is the

Figure 5.3 *Generalisation hierarchy (MERISE).*

Figure 5.4 *Specialisation hierarchy (MERISE).*

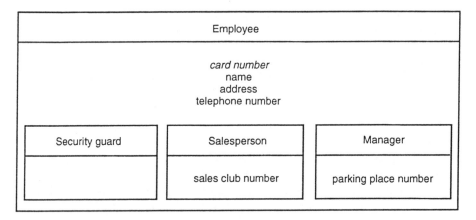

Figure 5.5 *Inheritance in a generalisation hierarchy. Attributes card number, name, address and telephone number inherited by manager, salesperson and security guard (MERISE).*

generic entity and manager, security guard and salesperson are specialised types of entity. The subtypes inherit the attributes card number, name, address and telephone number from the generic entity employee.

The diagram also shows attributes that subtypes possess exclusively and do not inherit; for example, the sales club number attribute of the salesperson subtype. Due to the type of diagram used however, inheritance can probably be represented on only one level to avoid excessive information.

SSADM

In SSADM, generalisation is not modelled by a special concept but is instead simulated by a binary relationship with a 1:1 cardinality ratio. The terms 'supertype of' and 'subtype of' may be used as the relationship link phrase. This is shown in Figure 5.6. However, this type of representation may meet problems if it is necessary, as in CASE tools based on SSADM such as Automate-plus (LBMS 1988), for each relationship to have a unique name.

The property inheritance concept is not defined in SSADM.

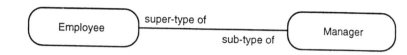

Figure 5.6 *Simulation of generalisation using 1:1 binary relationships: manager is a subtype of employee (SSADM).*

EXCLUSION AND EXHAUSTION

Definitions

In a generalisation hierarchy, there are two important types of restrictions modelled by the exclusion and exhaustion concepts. *Exclusion* refers to the situation where subtypes are a partition of the supertype. That is, where an instance of one subtype cannot also be an instance of another subtype. Other terms often used are *disjoint* or *non-overlapping* subtypes.

Secondly, *exhaustion* refers to the situation where the subtype instances consist of *all* the supertype instances. A non-exhaustive hierarchy is one where a supertype instance may exist that is not an instance of one of the defined subtypes. This may occur where it is unnecessary, for a particular model, to define all the possible subtypes that may exist for a given supertype.

IE

IE can specify, for a group of subtypes, whether an entity instance: (1) can exist as one of several subtypes (non-exclusive or overlapping), (2) can exist as only one subtype (exclusive), or (3) may or may not be one of the subtypes (non-exhaustive).

To represent exclusion, a box divided with solid lines is drawn and the names of the subtypes are written inside each division. If some subtypes are non-exclusive, a dashed line is used to divide the box with the names of the subtypes inside each division. If the subtypes are non-exhaustive, one of the divisions is blank. Figure 5.7 shows an example of a generalisation hierarchy with these different restrictions applied to the subtypes.

In Figure 5.7, the meaning is that an employee may be one of either manager, salesperson or security guard. As a security guard, an employee can be assigned to buildings, car parks, both or none of these (non-exhaustive).

When the subtyping is complex, IE uses a decomposition diagram to represent the subsets. In this type of diagram, a dot is used to represent exclusive subsets, as shown in Figure 5.8. IE also employs a conditional indicator to capture further meaning. This denotes that an entity instance *may* be one of the defined subtypes, but if it is, it is exclusive, as shown in Figure 5.9.

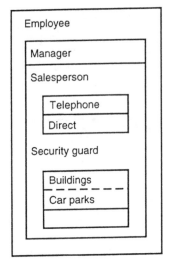

Figure 5.7   Entity employee showing exclusion and exhaustion between its subtypes (IE).

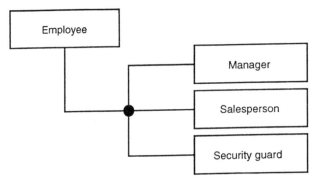

Figure 5.8   An employee can be only one of a manager, salesperson or security guard (IE).

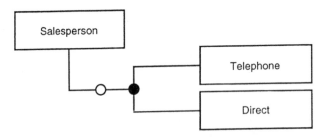

Figure 5.9   A salesperson does not necessarily have to be a telephone or a direct salesperson, but if so, cannot be both (IE).

AGGREGATION

Definition

Aggregation is an abstraction process which forms a higher-level entity type (*aggregate object*) from component entity, attribute and relationship types (Smith and Smith 1977). Aggregation establishes the 'part-of' association between the component objects and the aggregate object.

Aggregation may be used where we want, for example, to group a set of objects together so that we may build a relationship between an entity and the group.

MEIN

MEIN provides the concept of *associative entity*, which is equivalent to a restricted meaning of aggregate object. An associative entity may be formed by considering a relationship as an entity, and its graphical representation is a rectangle enclosing the relationship symbol, as shown in Figure 5.10. This shows that the relationship between supplier and part can be treated as the associative entity supply, which means that attributes, as in the figure, or entities, can be related directly to supply.

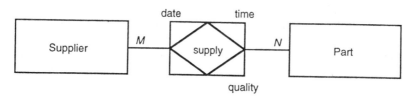

Figure 5.10 *Associative entity supply, aggregating the supplier:part relationship (MEIN).*

RULE

We use the term 'rule' to apply very generally to any restriction which may be applied to the values taken by the basic concepts of entity, attribute and relationship, either singly or in combination. We omit exclusion and exhaustion as these apply only to generalisation hierarchies.

As we mentioned in Chapter 1 in the discussion on information modelling, rules are an underdeveloped part of methods which are currently the subject of research

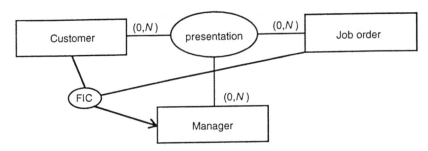

Figure 5.11 *Functional integrity constraint on entity manager (MERISE).*

effort. To give an idea of the concept, however, we briefly discuss the rules provided by the methods.

MERISE

MERISE defines one rule only, the functional integrity constraint, abbreviated as FIC (Rochfeld 1987; Collongues *et al.* 1989). An FIC applies to a relationship and is used to indicate that one of the entities linked to the relationship is entirely defined by the others. By the term 'entirely defined' MERISE means functionally determined, in the sense that a given instance of the relationship uniquely identifies one entity instance.

The FIC enables MERISE to model the multiple relationship example discussed in Chapter 4 in the cardinality restriction section, and the solution is shown in Figure 5.11. An FIC is represented by a small circle with the name 'FIC' written inside and arcs drawn to it from the source entity(ies), with an arrow drawn towards the target entity.

The meaning of Figure 5.11 is that a pair of instances, one from customer and one from job order (source entities) uniquely determines one instance of manager (target entity).

SSADM

In SSADM, an entity instance participating in a relationship may exclude its participation from other relationships. This is defined as an *exclusive relationship* (SSADM, 1990). Exclusive relationships can be grouped if the relationships have the same common entity. The relationships in the group must be all mandatory or all optional. For any instance of the common entity, only one of the relationships in a group may exist.

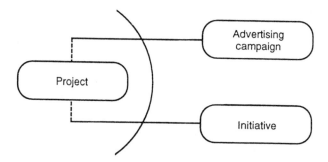

Figure 5.12 *Optional exclusive relationship group (SSADM).*

Exclusive relationships are graphically represented by an arc crossing the edges involved in the relevant relationships. Figure 5.12 shows an example of an optional exclusive group, with the meaning that a project may be related to either an advertising campaign or an initiative, but not both. Optional relationships are graphically represented, as usual for SSADM, by a dashed line.

SUMMARY

Although there are correspondences for generalisation, all methods have significant differences for the concepts discussed in this chapter. Table 5.2 shows the coverage of the methods for all concepts discussed. The graphical representations of the generalisation and inheritance concepts are summarised in Table 5.3, those of aggregation in Table 5.4 and exclusion, exhaustion and rule in Table 5.5.

Table 5.2 *Generalisation, inheritance, exclusion and exhaustion, aggregation and rule*

	Method			
Concept	**IE**	**MERISE**	**MEIN**	**SSADM**
Generalisation	yes	yes	yes	simulation
Exclusion and exhaustion	yes	–	–	–
Property inheritance	–	yes	yes	–
Multiple inheritance	–	–	–	–
Aggregation	–	–	yes	–
Rule	–	FIC	–	exclusive relationship

Table 5.3   Graphical representation of generalisation and inheritance

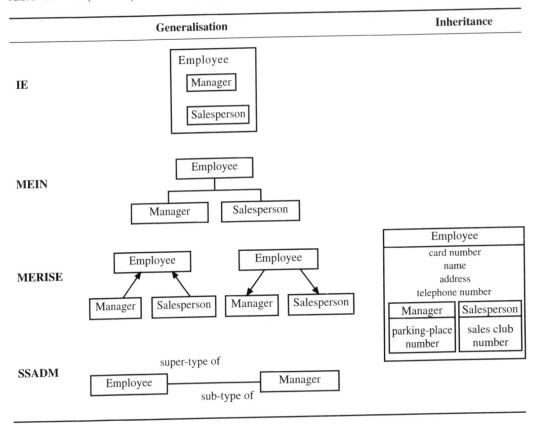

Table 5.4   Graphical representation of aggregation

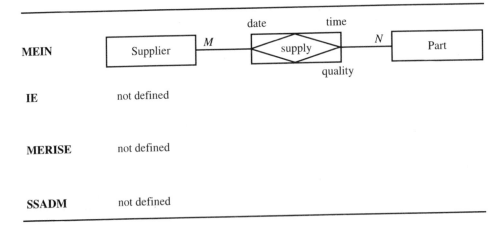

Table 5.5 Graphical representation of exclusion, exhaustion and rules

Method	Rule	Graphical representation
IE	Mutual exclusive subtypes	
	Entity type can be of several subtypes	
	Entity type **may** be or may not be one of the subtypes	
MEIN	No rule defined	
MERISE	Functional integrity constraint	
SSADM	Exclusive relationships	

Differences for all concepts

Significant differences between the methods exist for the concepts. SSADM simulates generalisation using binary relationships, which is ambiguous as it may be interpreted as a relationship between entities instead of between supertype and subtype.

Property inheritance is allowed by only MERISE and MEIN, and no method allows multiple inheritance.

Only IE provides the exclusion and exhaustion concepts that apply to the generalisation hierarchy. MEIN is the only method that allows aggregation, but in a restricted version, only allowing a relationship to be treated an entity. MERISE and SSADM provide one rule each, concerning different situations.

CONCLUSIONS

Reference framework concepts

- *Generalisation.* IE, MEIN and MERISE allow this while SSADM simulates it.

- *Property inheritance.* Only MEIN and MERISE allow this.

- *Multiple inheritance.* No method allows this.

- *Exclusion and exhaustion.* Only IE allows this.

- *Aggregation.* Only MEIN allows this.

- *Rule.* MERISE and SSADM provide one (different) rule each.

Method scope

- No one method allows all the relevant concepts of generalisation, property inheritance, exclusion and exhaustion applied to generalisation hierarchies.

- No method provides the concept of multiple inheritance discussed briefly at the beginning of the chapter.

- Methods provide different types of rule.

Modelling guidance

The associative entity provided by MEIN involves a modelling choice, as it is necessary to decide between relating attributes to an associative entity or using the relationship attribute concept. Another choice concerns IE, which provides two graphical means to represent exclusion and exhaustion.

In both these cases the quality criterion of *non-complexity* might form part of guidance, as it is concerned with reducing diagrammatic complexity in models.

Chapter 6

CASE STUDY – DISCUSSION AND STRUCTURE MODEL SOLUTION

This chapter is concerned with applying the modelling concepts we have discussed in previous chapters to building an information model based on the case study, and it consists of two sections:

I.   In the first section, detailed comments are made on a range of topics which will assist the student to understand the case study and its structure model solution.

II. In the second section, the structure model solution is presented. This consists of (a) annotated case study text for requirements tracing, (b) graphical structure models for each of the four methods, (c) entity–attribute list.

I. COMMENTS ON CASE STUDY SOLUTION

In this section we discuss several topics which cover general issues in building structure models, as well as making comments on various aspects of the specific models presented in Section II.

The topics covered are:

- general principles that apply when building structure models;

- how to build a structure model in practice;

- specific principles used to build the case study structure model;

- specific points from the case study structure model;

- individual method case study solutions;

- comments on the entity–attribute list;

- omissions from the case study structure model.

GENERAL PRINCIPLES FOR STRUCTURE MODELLING

Quality criteria

When we build an information model our primary aim is to model user requirements completely and correctly. However, to do this we need more than just the concepts and viewpoints provided by the method. This is because methods usually provide more than one concept that may be used to model a given situation, and guidance is often required to make a modelling choice. Guidance is important as it helps to avoid modelling errors, standardises model production and assists developer communication.

For example, MERISE and MEIN provide both the binary and the *n*-ary relationship concepts to model a multiple relationship, as described in Chapter 4.

In addition to information concerning such concepts and their use, guidance may take the form of *quality criteria* such as non-complexity and naturalness, briefly discussed in Chapters 4 and 5. Within the essentially creative activity of information modelling, quality criteria may be applied by trying to ensure that they are met by the evolving model.

During information modelling, when we make a choice between concepts, we may base our choice on, for example, whether a certain concept is more complex than another, or whether a certain concept is more or less natural and therefore more or less suitable for model validation.

The decisions that we make are subjective, based on the weightings we attach to the criteria and on the fact that criteria may often interact or conflict, but an awareness of their relevance to the production of a high-quality model may assist the designer in making consistent decisions.

Three common criteria are:

1. *Precision*. Method concepts should not be used if they do not model a situation precisely. For example, the binary relationship concept should not be used to model multiple relationships, as described in Chapter 4, if identifiers cannot be precisely defined.

2. *Non-complexity*. Method concepts should be chosen that are diagrammatically simple. An example concerns the choice between associative entity and relationship attribute discussed in Chapter 5.

3. *Naturalness*. Method concepts should be chosen that correspond to concepts in the user's organisation. The choice between the binary and the *n*-ary relationship concept is affected by this criterion as well as precision. We may note that this criterion may conflict with the choice of user-centred or developer-centred models.

User-centred or developer-centred

Should a structure model be:

- user-centred – primarily for communication between developer and user?

- developer-centred – primarily as a basis for detailed design and for communication between developers?

A user-centred model emphasises the role of the model in validation, whereby the user can understand the model and detect any errors or omissions. A developer-centred model focuses on the role of the model as a precisely expressed formalism (perhaps to be processed by a machine) that can be used for design and implementation and is primarily understandable to developers.

Two structure models built from the same case study may be quite different if each has been built with a different role in mind. For example, a developer-centred model typically represents case study elements in a flat, non-hierarchical structure, while a user-centred model requires levels of detail, so that the user can understand the model without getting lost in too much detail.

Another difference is that a developer-centred model often emphasises data representation issues, while a user-centred model is concerned with *what* objects are in the model, not *how* they are to be represented in data.

The different roles affect the level of emphasis on attributes, as a developer is interested in data representation and thus tends to use attributes instead of entities, subtypes and relationships. Attributes are also simpler to deal with as they are a uniform type of representation. In contrast, a user may be interested in a highly visible graphical model and so a user-centred model emphasises graphical entity, subtype and relationship modelling, with attributes on a lower level of detail, in a textual format.

In recent years, the emphasis has moved from developer-centred towards user-centred, and many current guidelines reflect this movement at different points. It is unsatisfactory to mix the two, as they are largely incompatible, and in this case study we produce a *user-centred* model.

Broad or narrow object definition

Two approaches that may be taken when deciding on the type of object to be included in a structure model are the *broad* and *narrow* approaches. They are based on the interpretation of the phrase 'object of interest' used in the definition of an entity.

Narrow approach

The narrow approach assumes that the purpose of the structure model is to act as a high level abstraction for a database or set of files that will form part of the eventual system. An 'object of interest' is thus one about which *information is to be recorded* in such a database, and duplication of this information should be avoided, as this would make an eventual database inefficient and might lead to inconsistency.

Broad approach

The broad approach assumes that the purpose of the structure model is to act as a high level abstraction for all the static part of the eventual system. The model will consider objects such as data input forms, reports, screen contents and intermediate data stores, as well as 'narrow approach' objects, as objects of interest.

The model will thus contain duplicated information: for example, a customer address may be recorded as an address attribute of a customer entity as well as an attribute of an entity representing a data input form concerning that customer.

We have used the *narrow* approach for building the structure model in this chapter.

Distinction between entities and attributes

A frequent problem encountered by the student is the nature of the distinction between entities and attributes. The question frequently asked, particularly before some modelling experience has been gained, is: should a given element be modelled as an entity or an attribute?

Guidelines

There is no general answer to this question, but there are several guidelines which may be used. However, the guidelines depend on whether a user-centred or a developer-centred model is being built. As we are building a user-centred model, then the guidelines that follow fit this type of model.

The most important guideline is that important information should not be modelled as attributes, as they are not very visible on the model. Attributes are on a lower level of refinement than entities, as they express detail about the entity. Typically, the majority of attributes are not shown on the graphical model but are documented in a textual format. They are thus less visible than entities so they may not be checked or validated very closely.

The second guideline applies to entity subtypes, which should not be modelled as attributes. The thinking here is that users distinguish between subtypes by their names, and this information may be lost if they are modelled using attributes. Although some guidelines recommend that subtypes should not be considered without their defining attributes, this is a rather data-centred view.

The third guideline is that information modelled in entity relationships should not be duplicated (or substituted) in entity attributes. This is both for visibility reasons and to avoid duplication. The fourth guideline is that where the values of an object clearly identify the instances of another object, then the first object is almost certainly an identifier (attribute) of the second object.

You will find further useful discussions of issues such as these in Coad (1992), Wintraecken (1990), Batini *et al.* (1992), Ter Bekke (1992) and Benyon (1990).

Case study

The case study has been written so that the number of attributes has been kept to a minimum. This is to reduce the length and complexity of the case study, so that when you read it you will find it quite easy to distinguish entities from attributes and you may wonder what all the fuss is about! However, in practice, it is common to find thirty or forty attributes for an entity and you may find it more difficult then.

HOW TO BUILD A STRUCTURE MODEL IN PRACTICE

Introduction

Here is some general advice to help you build a structure model in practice. The key point is to be systematic and to proceed gradually, building up layers of detail.

We assume that you are working from user requirements expressed in a textual form.

Although the advice is presented in the form of a sequence of ten steps, you should be aware the the steps are essentially iterative, so you will often need information from a later step to help you with a current step!

As you model a particular element from your source text it often helps in later completeness checking if you underline, tick or in some way highlight the element in the text.

Steps

1. Decide on (a) user- or developer-centred, (b) narrow or broad approach.

2. Write down a list of likely entities. Remove redundancies.

3. Identify generalisation hierarchies from the entity list.

4. Build a rough graphical model by drawing (a) generalisation hierarchies, (b) binary relationships for relevant entities.

5. Build a rough entity–attribute list emphasising entity identifiers and important attributes. Check the semantics of your entities and that you do not have redundant or missing entities.

6. Add relationship names and constraints to all relationships.

7. Check $M:N$ relationships for the presence of (a) intersection entities, (b) multiple relationships. Remodel if necessary.

8. Add all attributes to the entity–attribute list and add their relationship constraints.

9. Check any ambiguities (there will be lots!), or assumptions you have made, in a validation session with your users.

10. Remodel or add further detail.

SPECIFIC PRINCIPLES USED TO BUILD THE CASE STUDY STRUCTURE MODELS

Introduction

To reduce the complexity and amount of detail in both the case study text and the model we used some specific principles to guide us, and it is useful for you to be aware of these.

Defaults

We have assumed default values for (entity) relationship constraints. The default for the cardinality constraint is 'many' while the default for the participation constraint is 'mandatory'. That is, unless there is information to the contrary in the case study text, we have assumed that a given entity relationship is many and mandatory from the direction of that entity.

Role names

Only a few role (relationship) names from the case study are shown in the model. In practice, however, all role names should be modelled as they enable users to check the semantics of relationships.

Attributes

Only those attributes are mentioned in the case study text which are sufficient to illustrate the different types of entity–attribute relationship. However, to provide more information concerning the semantics of the entities many identifiers have been assumed and are shown in the entity–attribute list. In practice, all identifiers and attributes would be required in the text or from validation.

SPECIFIC POINTS IN THE STRUCTURE MODELS

Here we discuss the modelling of specific elements of the case study that we feel would benefit from further explanation.

Entities

Granularity

An entity instance may represent a single object in the organisation or a set of similar objects which the user does not wish to distinguish. This concept is termed the granularity of the entity.

In the case study, the part entity differs from other entities in the sense that an instance of part models a collection of parts of the same type. For example, an instance might represent a collection of grade 000 sandpaper. The key fact which gives us this information about part is the presence of the quantity attribute. Thus the instance representing sandpaper may have a quantity attribute value of 100.

Concrete entities

Concrete entities, such as supplier, customer and employee, have instances which represent concrete objects.

Abstract entities

Abstract entities fall into two categories: those which are information-related and those which are not.

Information-related entities

These entities, such as customer account, bill, receipt, reminder, payment, job proposal, job order, complaint, purchase order and supplier account, represent abstractions which exist solely to bear information.

They are instantiated whenever, for example, a bill is sent to Aquaduct by a supplier, a reminder is sent to a customer, an update is made to an account or a purchase order is created for sending to a supplier. They do *not* represent the information-bearing material objects such as paper forms, cheques and letters which are 'external' representations, as input, output or temporary storage media, of the abstractions.

As we adopt the narrow approach to structure modelling, information related entities will not contain redundant information, and thus the abstractions they represent may be considered as abstractions of the information borne by the material objects.

For example, an instance of the customer reminder entity consists only of a reminder number, the reminder amount and the date the reminder was sent, and not detail such as customer address, account number and other information which would exist on the reminder material object (which may be a letter) in the organisation. This may be seen in the entity–attribute list.

Non-information-related entities

These entities, including department, section, presentation, project, initiative, advertising campaign and supply have instances which represent abstract objects in the organisation which do not exist solely to bear information.

Intersection entity

We briefly mentioned the topic of intersection entity in previous chapters, where it was presented as an alternative way of modelling the situation where a relationship has attributes. We now discuss its use in the two methods that describe it explicitly.

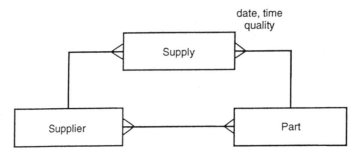

Figure 6.1 *Intersection entity supply, dependent on entities supplier and part (IE).*

IE

An intersection entity, supply, is shown in Figure 6.1, each instance of which represents both a supplier and a part. The meaning of the entity in this example is that the supplier is approved to supply the part. It is dependent on the entities supplier and part as it has no meaning if either supplier or part does not exist.

A semantic reason for creating an intersection entity exists where a relationship between two entities is required to have attributes and the relationship attribute concept is not present in the method.

The intersection entity supply in Figure 6.1 is shown with the attributes date and time, modelling this information about supplier approval. The quality attribute records information concerned with the quality of the part supplied by the supplier.

The usual conditions for the existence of an intersection entity are that the two entities on which it is dependent have an $M:N$ cardinality ratio. Figure 6.1 shows that the supplier:part relationship is $M:N$ and also shows that the cardinality ratios of the supplier:supply and part:supply relationships are $1:N$. These two relationships are equivalent in meaning to the $M:N$ supplier:part relationship. This means that the supplier:part relationship is redundant and can be omitted, as it is on the IE case study solution in Figure 6.3.

SSADM

The *link entity* in SSADM corresponds to the concept of intersection entity and is graphically represented in a similar manner. It is often used to 'resolve' an $M:N$ relationship into a link entity with two $1:N$ relationships with the entities on which the link entity depends.

Modelling intersection entities

It is not immediately obvious when reading the case study text that supply and customer account are intersection entities. However, it is usually the case that it is the $M:N$ relationship between the base entities, on which the intersection entity depends, that is mentioned, and modelled, first.

For example, in paragraph 1 the customer and job order relationship is mentioned, and it is not until paragraph 3 that the customer account entity and its relationship to these base entities is mentioned.

Multiple relationships

There are two multiple relationships, presentation and complaint, and the cardinality constraints that exist between all participating entities should be noted in conjunction with the discussion in Chapter 4. The case study text has been written so that these are easy to find, and they are in paragraphs 4 and 5.

Note that the cardinalities of the participating entities in the presentation and complaint multiple relationships are different. For complaint, any participating entity may have many complaints, but for presentation, a manager may only give one presentation.

Relationships

You should note that the semantics of the supply relationship between entities supplier and part are not that a supplier has supplied a particular part, but that the supplier is approved to supply that part. The fact that a part actually will be (or has been) supplied is recorded via the purchase order entity and its relationships with supplier and part.

Relationship cardinality modelling

It is common to find modelling guidelines that suggest the resolution of $M:N$ entity relationships into an intersection entity and two $1:N$ relationships. In addition, some guidelines suggest that 1:1 entity relationships are 'wrong', and should be modelled in some other way, perhaps as entity–attribute relationships.

Such guidelines are very general, however, and applying them indiscriminately might result in incorrect modelling. If all $M:N$ relationships were resolved as suggested, then, for example, the single combination entity complaint, which expresses the combination of participating entities in the multiple relationship complaint, would not be modelled.

If 1:1 relationships were to be modelled as entity–attribute relationships, then the presentation:manager 1:1 relationship, for SSADM, IE and MEIN, involved in the presentation multiple relationship, would need to be changed so that, for example, the manager entity became an attribute. However, this would remove manager as a subtype.

Both of these guidelines perhaps spring from a developer-centred rather than a user-centred viewpoint. The resolution guideline seems oriented only to binary rather than to higher-degree relationships.

INDIVIDUAL METHOD SOLUTIONS

We now make some points concerning the differences between the individual methods and their case study solutions. In general, Figures 6.2–6.5 show that the solutions differ with respect to generalisation, multiple relationships and relationship constraints.

Intersection entity supply

The choice between a relationship attribute and an intersection entity in MERISE was based on the complexity criterion, judging that the relationship attribute was less complex. SSADM and IE can only model this with an intersection entity.

Multiple relationships

IE and SSADM require combination entities with binary relationships to model these, while MERISE and MEIN can use the n-ary relationship. However, MEIN cannot model the semantics of presentation with the n-ary relationship and instead must use binary relationships.

Generalisation

Generalisation in SSADM is effectively limited to only one level. Only MERISE provides graphical inheritance.

Relationship constraints

Each method has its own approach to the graphical representation of these. MEIN does not have the relationship participation constraint.

COMMENTS ON THE ENTITY–ATTRIBUTE LIST

The list consists of all entities arranged alphabetically, showing their attributes and attribute relationship constraints.

Defaults

The defaults assumed for attribute relationship constraints are:

- for identifiers, one:one; mandatory (from the direction of the entity);
- for non-identifying attributes, many:one; mandatory (from the direction of the entity).

Case study attributes

Attributes that are mentioned in the case study text are shown in bold type. However, as stated above, many attributes are listed which are not mentioned, to reduce complexity, but they have been provided in the list to help understand the semantics of their entities. It sometimes helps to understand the semantics of an entity by visualising its data representation. You can do this by instantiating the identifier and each of the entity attributes with a value to represent an instance of the entity.

It will be noted that the names of many identifiers consist partly of 'number': for example, account number, bill number. It is usual to have this type of identifier, rather than a natural one originating from an entity attribute (such as customer name or supplier reference number) to avoid problems of non-uniqueness.

Intersection entities and multiple relationships

Note that the identifiers of the intersection entities supply and customer account, and the multiple relationship combination entities complaint and presentation are composite, made up of the identifiers of their 'base' or participating entities.

Generalisation hierarchy – employee

This is shown by indenting subtypes underneath their supertypes, and indicating inheritance of supertype attributes. Only MEIN and MERISE provide inheritance.

OMISSIONS FROM THE STRUCTURE MODEL

To keep the case study solution manageable in terms of size, whilst providing a description of a realistic situation, we have found it necessary to avoid modelling some of the more detailed areas of the case study text.

It is often found, in dealing with user requirements such as the case study text, that there are mentions of context which are useful to assist understanding but which are not intended to be modelled. There may be an accompanying note which delineates the boundaries between areas that are to be inside or outside the eventual system.

Our aim has been to provide a case study that will show practical and integrated examples of the modelling concepts in the methods; we do not necessarily aim to show how all the detail of a case study may be modelled.

However, despite the above reasons, it can still be confusing for the student to be confronted with a model that does not include all the elements in the related case study. The question may be asked: why has a certain case study element not been modelled? Is it because it is context, is it implied by some other part of the model, is it not required as there are other examples of this modelling concept, or did the case study compiler forget about it?

To address this last point, we list below the areas which we have not modelled, with reasons, indicating the relevant paragraphs.

- It is unnecessary to model Aquaduct as an instance of an entity, for example, organisation, as the entity would have only one instance and it would be strictly necessary to relate every other entity to organisation. This would add great complexity to the model (paragraph 1).

- Although a job proposal may eventually become a job order, the relationship between them has been omitted as the relationship is not used by any process (paragraphs 1 and 7).

- Potential or existing customers could be different subtypes of the customer entity. Several potential subtypes have been omitted as there are other examples of the concept (paragraph 1).

- Customer details have been assumed to be the customer attributes listed in the entity–attribute list (paragraph 1).

- Amended proposal could be a subtype of job proposal (paragraph 1).

- Marketing department could be a subtype of department, prestigious projects could be subtypes of project, school projects and artistic festivals could be subtypes of initiative (paragraph 3).

- Dissatisfied customer could be a subtype of customer (paragraph 4).

- We don't wish to record information about literature or hot line telephone numbers as this is context information (paragraph 4).

- New staff could be a subtype of employee (paragraph 5).

- Reviews of organisation procedures is context description (paragraph 5).

- Rejected request and approved, rejected or closed proposals may be subtypes of job request and job proposal respectively (paragraph 6).

- Job costing section could be a subtype of section. First payment could be a subtype of customer payment (paragraph 7).

- Cost of labour is assumed to be an attribute, rather than an entity, which is calculated outside the eventual system (paragraph 7).

- Approved supplier could be a subtype of supplier (paragraph 8).

- Accountant could be a subtype of employee (paragraph 10).

II. CASE STUDY SOLUTION – STRUCTURE MODEL

This section presents the solution to the structure part of the case study. The solution is in three parts:

1. The case study text from Chapter 1 is repeated with the addition of detail to make requirements tracing between the text and the structure model easier. We do this by listing, under each numbered text paragraph, the entities, attributes and relationships which are introduced in that paragraph.

2. The graphical forms of the structure models are presented for each of the four methods: the LDS of SSADM, the CPM of MERISE, and the entity–relationship diagrams of IE and MEIN.

3. An entity–attribute list showing entities, their associated attributes and relationship constraints is provided. As stated in Chapter 2, there is no standard form in which this type of information is presented, with methods variously referring to concepts such as a data dictionary, encyclopaedia and data inventory.

    For this reason, as well as to avoid detailed repetition, just one list is provided rather than four, with notes on the main differences between the methods.

CASE STUDY TEXT

The case study from Chapter 1 is given below, listing the concepts to be found in each paragraph.

Aquaduct plumber case study

(1) Potential or existing customers contact Aquaduct with their needs and, after ascertaining customer details, a job proposal is sent to them. On customer acceptance the proposal, or an amended version, becomes a job order, and a manager is assigned to the job order. Some job orders have several customers and a set of related job orders may be classed as a project.

- **Entities:** *customer, job proposal, job order, manager, project*

- **Relationships:** *customer:job proposal, customer: job order, manager:job order, job order:project*

(2) There are several types of employee, including managers, salespersons and security guards. Employee details including card number, names, address and telephone numbers are recorded; card number is unique and is mandatory, while the other details are optional; telephones are shared and several employees may have the same address. In addition, managers have a parking place number and salespersons have a sales club number. Security guards may be assigned to both buildings and car parks, but salespersons may be either telephone or direct salespersons. Customers are assigned to exactly two salespersons and employees work with other employees in teams.

- **Entities:** *employee* with subtypes *manager, salesperson, security guard; security guard* with subtypes *buildings, car parks; salesperson* with subtypes *telephone, direct*

- **Attributes:** *employee (card number, names, address, telephone numbers); manager (parking place number); salesperson (sales club number)*

- **Relationships:** *employee:employee, customer:salesperson*

(3) A customer holds an Aquaduct account for each relevant job order; the account belongs to the customer. Certain projects are very prestigious and the marketing department may plan an advertising campaign which publicises that project and the involvement of Aquaduct. Alternatively, a project may be publicised by sponsoring a local initiative, such as a school project or artistic festival, but it may not be publicised by both a campaign and an initiative. A campaign or initiative concern only one project and vice versa.

- **Entities:** *customer account, advertising campaign, initiative*

- **Relationships:** *customer:customer account, job order:customer account, project: advertising campaign, project:initiative*

(4) A customer may be dissatisfied, as happens from time to time, and Aquaduct are proud of their complaints procedure which they set up to deal with this situation. This is described in the literature which is sent to every customer concerning a job order and involves a hot line telephone number for customers to phone. Complaints information recorded concerns the customer, the job order and the department concerned. Departments comprise sections and section names are unique only within their department.

- **Entities:** *complaint, department, section*

- **Attributes:** *section (section name)*

- **Relationships:** *customer:job order:department (complaint), department:section*

(5) Apart from the benefit to customer relations provided by this procedure, Aquaduct find that complaints constitute a source of information that is useful for inducting new staff, as well as leading to reviews of organisation procedures. Information is recorded concerning presentations which may be made where managers talk about the experience of job orders with different customers. A manager can make a presentation about only one job order and one customer.

- **Entities:** *presentation*
- **Relationships:** *customer:job order:manager (presentation)*

The activities that are carried out at the beginning and end of a job order, and those activities concerning payments, may be summarised as follows:

(6) *Job request.* Customers make job requests to Aquaduct, and in response the request may be rejected, or a job proposal may be written and sent to the customers. The customer may approve or reject the proposal. If it is rejected the proposal is closed.

- **Entities:** *job request*
- **Relationships:** *customer:job request*

(7) *Job proposal.* A job proposal must specify the parts needed, their prices and the cost of labour, obtained from the job costing section. The proposal is sent to the customer with a job order form. If the customer approves the proposal, the customer must sign the job order form and make the first payment for the job order. Aquaduct sends the proposal and a receipt for the first payment to the customer.

- **Entities:** *part, customer payment*
- **Attributes:** *job proposal (labour cost), part (price)*
- **Relationships:** *customer account:customer payment, job proposal:part, job order:part*

(8) *Job order.* When the job order is signed, the file of parts is checked. If parts are not in stock, indicated by the quantities, a purchase order is prepared and sent to an approved supplier. The date and time when a supplier was approved for a part is recorded. The supplier must supply bills and receipts for any supplied parts, which are used to update the supplier account. A supplier should have an account eventually, but not necessarily initially. The parts file is updated with any new parts.

- **Entities:** *purchase order, supplier, bill, receipt, supplier account*

- **Attributes:** *part (quantity), supplier–part (date, time)*
- **Relationships:** *part:supplier, part:purchase order, purchase order:supplier, supplier:supplier account, supplier account:bill, supplier account:receipt*

(9) Customer account. When a job order is signed, the customer account is updated with customer details. At the end of the month a reminder is sent to a customer to pay a certain amount. On receipt of payment, the payment is checked against the customer account, which is then updated.

- **Entities:** *customer reminder*
- **Attributes:** *customer reminder (amount)*
- **Relationships:** *customer account:customer reminder*

(10) When a job has finished and the customer has made all the payments, an end-of-job report will be sent to the customer. In addition, the account balance is elaborated and sent, along with customer details, to the accountant.

(11) *Supplier account.* The suppliers should send reminders every end of month to Aquaduct. Aquaduct checks the supplier account and, if valid, makes a payment to the supplier. The supplier account is updated. If the reminder amount is inconsistent with the supplier account, then the supplier account balance is elaborated and sent, along with supplier details, to the accountant.

- **Entities:** *supplier reminder, supplier payment*
- **Attributes:** *supplier reminder (amount)*
- **Relationships:** *supplier account:supplier reminder, supplier account:supplier payment*

(12) *Parts file.* At the end of every month, a report about transactions on parts is produced and sent to the accountant. If an error exists in the report it is redone. To monitor part quality, information may be kept for each part supplied by a supplier, recording ratings and the date of the ratings.

- **Entities:** *supplier–part*
- **Attributes:** *supplier–part (quality)*

GRAPHICAL STRUCTURE MODELS

Figures 6.2–6.5 show the graphical structure models for SSADM, IE, MERISE and MEIN for the case study.

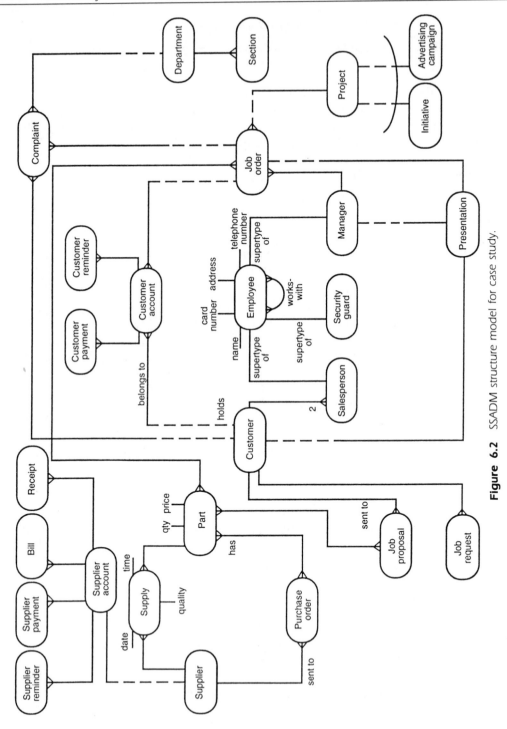

Figure 6.2 SSADM structure model for case study.

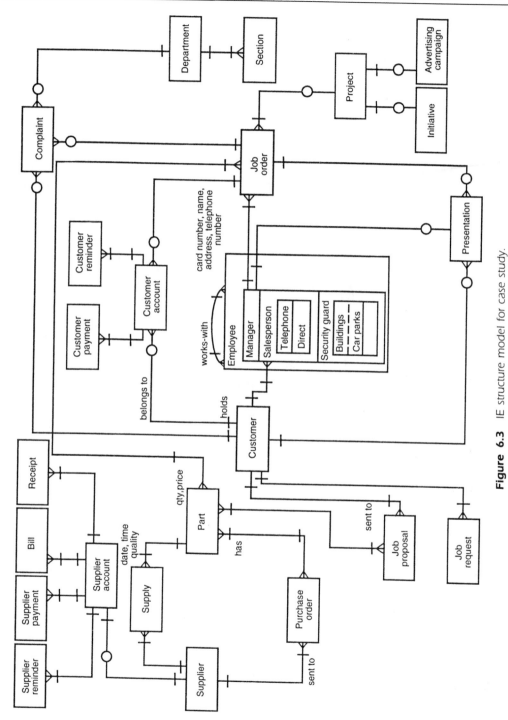

Figure 6.3 IE structure model for case study.

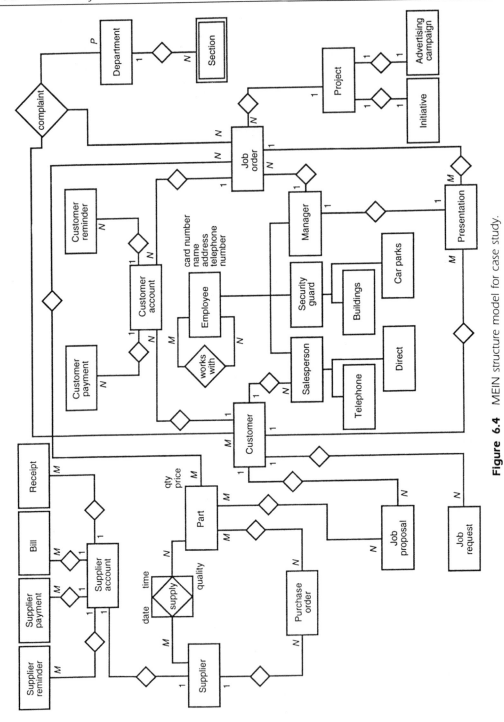

Figure 6.4 MEIN structure model for case study.

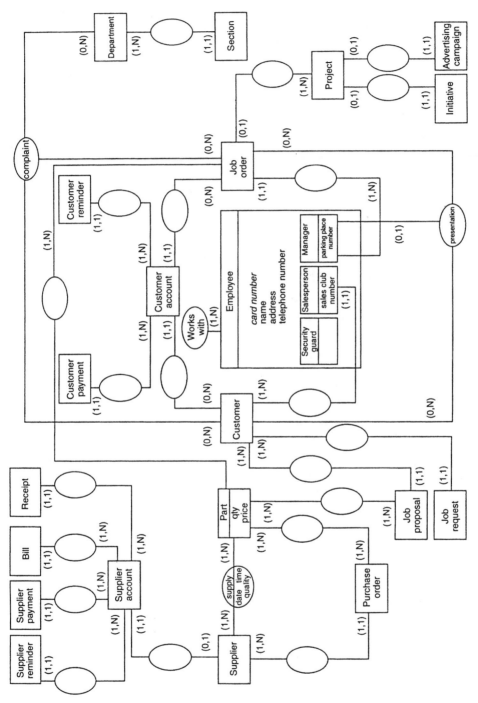

Figure 6.5 MERISE structure model for case study.

ENTITY–ATTRIBUTE LIST

Entity	Attribute	Constraints
1. advertising campaign	name budget agency name date	
2. bill	bill number part number amount date	
3. complaint	customer number/job order number/ department name date time	
4. customer	customer number name address telephone number	
5. customer account	customer number/job order number credit limit balance	
6. customer payment	payment number amount date	
7. customer reminder	reminder number date **amount**	
8. department	department name	
9. employee	**card number** **name** **address** (house/apt, street, postcode) **telephone number**	one:many, optional optional many:many, optional
manager	**parking place number** *(inherits employee attributes)*	
salesperson	**sales club number** *(inherits employee attributes)*	
telephone direct		
security guard buildings car parks	*(inherits employee attributes)*	
10. initiative	initiative name	
11. job order	job order number job name budget date	

Entity	Attribute	Constraints
12. job proposal	<u>job proposal number</u> **labour cost**	
13. job request	<u>job request number</u> date	
14. part	<u>part number</u> **price** **quantity**	
15. presentation	<u>customer number/job order number/ card number</u> date time	
16. project	<u>project number</u> date	
17. purchase order	<u>purchase order number</u> amount date	
18. receipt	<u>receipt number</u> part number amount date	
19. section	<u>department name/**section name**</u>	
20. supplier	<u>supplier number</u> name address telephone number	
21. supplier account	<u>supplier account number</u> credit limit balance	
22. supplier reminder	<u>supplier reminder number</u> date **amount**	
23. supplier payment	<u>supplier payment number</u> amount date	
24. supply	<u>supplier number/part number</u> **date** **time** **quality (rating, date)**	one:many; optional

Notes
1. Identifiers are underlined. Bold type indicates that the attribute is explicitly mentioned in the case study text.
2. Inheritance is not provided in IE or SSADM. Supertype attributes must be duplicated on their subtypes.
3. Composite attributes are provided only in MEIN.
4. Attribute relationship constraints are not provided in MEIN or MERISE, and are restricted in IE and SSADM (see Chapter 2).
5. Combination entities presentation and complaint do not exist for those methods which can model them with the *n*-ary relationship concept.

Chapter 7

METHOD COMPARISON – STRUCTURE MODEL

In this chapter we discuss the correspondences and differences between the structure modelling concepts in the methods. Table 7.1 summarises the reference framework concepts and the method correspondences. The entry (yes) means that the method is restricted in its scope for this concept.

Table 7.1 *Summary of scope of structure modelling IE, MERISE, MEIN and SSADM*

Concept	Method			
	IE	MERISE	MEIN	SSADM
Entity	yes	yes	yes	yes
Attribute	yes	yes	yes	yes
Identifier	yes	yes	yes	yes
Attribute relationship cardinality	yes	–	–	(yes)
Attribute relationship optionality	(yes)	–	–	(yes)
Binary relationship	yes	yes	yes	yes
Cardinality constraint	yes	yes	yes	yes
Participation constraint	yes	yes	–	yes
Relationship attribute	–	yes	yes	–
N-ary relationship	–	yes	yes	–
Generalisation	yes	yes	yes	–
Property inheritance	–	yes	yes	–
Multiple inheritance	–	–	–	–
Exclusion	yes	–	–	–
Exhaustion	yes	–	–	–
Aggregation	–	–	(yes)	–
Rule	–	FIC	–	exclusive relationship

REFERENCE FRAMEWORK CONCEPTS

Correspondences

All methods provide the concepts of *entity, attribute, identifier, binary relationship* and *cardinality constraint*.

Differences

Attribute relationship cardinality and *optionality* are not defined at all in MEIN or MERISE, and are restricted in IE and SSADM.

MEIN does not provide the *participation constraint. Relationships with attributes* are provided only by MEIN and MERISE. Only MEIN and MERISE provide the *n-ary relationship*.

Under the general concept of generalisation, SSADM does not provide *generalisation*, and only MERISE and MEIN provide *property inheritance. Exclusion* and *exhaustion* are only provided by IE. No method provides *multiple inheritance*.

For *aggregation*, only a restricted version is provided by the associative entity in MEIN.

CONCLUSIONS

No one method provides all the reference framework concepts that we have discussed. The methods have basic correspondences in that they all provide the concepts of entity, attribute, cardinality constraint and binary relationship.

However, for the other reference framework concepts, there are significant differences between the methods.

Generalisation

There are major differences in the generalisation concept, including inheritance. Although it may be argued that attributes can be used to simulate generalisation hierarchies, in Chapter 6 we argued against such a developer-centred view.

N-ary relationship

An important difference is in the provision of the *n*-ary relationship concept. However, no one method has an advantage when modelling multiple relationships.

As we showed in Chapter 4, where we discussed cardinality and participation variations, there is at least one situation which a method cannot model using the *n*-ary relationship concept.

Modelling guidance

Each method should consider whether to provide more explicit guidance, including quality criteria, to the designer for selecting the correct modelling approach to situations such as different types of multiple relationship and relationships with attributes. Such guidance can help to standardise different models produced by different designers.

Part III

PROCESS MODEL

Part III discusses the reference framework concepts and viewpoints provided for process modelling by the methods Information Engineering, SSADM, MEIN and MERISE.

We shall discuss the reference framework in the methods and then present the case study solutions, concluding with a method comparison in Chapter 13, where we summarise the correspondences between the methods and the reference framework, discuss major differences and method scope and also discuss points arising from the application of quality criteria to process models.

Chapter 8 discusses the concepts provided by the data flow diagram (DFD) of SSADM and MEIN, with their process models for the Aquaduct case study described in Chapter 9.

Chapter 10 discusses the concepts and viewpoints provided by IE, MERISE and SSADM, and their case study process models are discussed in Chapters 11 and 12.

Splitting the description of the methods in this way enables us to consider the simpler models, without control structures, in Chapter 8, leaving models with control structures to Chapter 10.

Reference framework

The reference framework concepts for the process model are external entity, process, event, data flow, data store and control structure.

The viewpoints of the reference framework, which define the concepts and their interrelationships that express a certain perspective over the model are decomposition, behavioural, data flow and state transition.

Process model components

The diagrams which comprise the process models of the methods are as follows:

Information Engineering	process decomposition diagram
	process dependency diagram
	process data flow diagram
SSADM	data flow diagram (DFD)
	entity life history (ELH)
MEIN	data flow diagram (DFD)
MERISE	flow diagram (FD)
	conceptual processing model (CPM)

Chapter 8

PROCESS MODELS WITHOUT CONTROL STRUCTURES

INTRODUCTION

Data flow diagram

This chapter is concerned with a comparison of the process modelling concepts of MEIN and SSADM, and the focus is on process modelling in the data flow diagram (DFD).

A DFD is a model of the part of the organisation under consideration viewed as an *information processing system*, showing the movement of information or material within the system and between the system and its environment. This meaning of the term 'system' is important in this chapter as several definitions are based on it.

A DFD consists of a context diagram, representing the system as one process and showing its environment, and intermediate level diagrams obtained when the context diagram is decomposed. Elementary processes occur on the lowest level diagrams, which cannot be decomposed further and which may have textual process specifications associated. The DFD thus provides different levels of detail, from the general to the more specific.

There are two types of DFD; the *physical* and the *logical* DFD. The physical DFD is used on the design level, and is concerned with how information and material are moved in a system, representing physical detail such as who carries out processes and where information is stored. The logical DFD is used on the analysis level, and is the one with which we are concerned, being concerned with what information is being moved.

Reference framework concepts

The process modelling reference framework concepts that we shall describe are external entity, process, event, data flow and data store.

EXTERNAL ENTITY

An external entity represents a source or destination of information in the environment of a system

External entities exist outside the boundary (the system boundary) of the part of the organisation under consideration, and can be persons, organisations or information systems. They are modelled to aid comprehension and to indicate system input and output. Further information about them is not recorded.

An example of an external entity in the Aquaduct case study is the job costing section, which is outside the boundary of the part of Aquaduct under consideration, and which receives information (a labour list) and returns additional information in the form of labour costs.

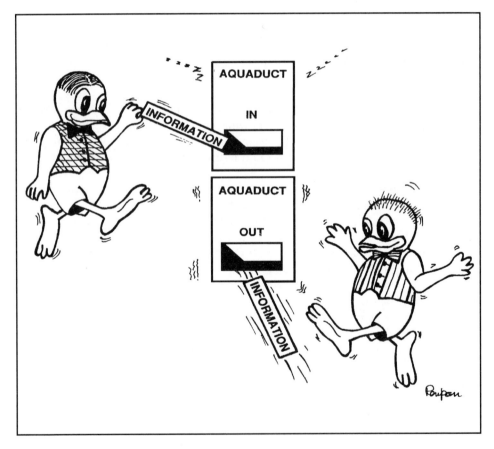

An external entity may be a source or a destination of information.

Figure 8.1   *External entity customer (MEIN).*

Figure 8.2   *Replicated external entity customer (SSADM).*

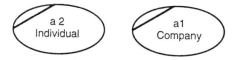

Figure 8.3   *Replicated decomposed external entities individual and company (SSADM).*

MEIN

For MEIN an external entity is defined in a similar way to the general definition above. It is graphically represented as a dark shadowed rectangle with its name written inside, as shown in Figure 8.1.

SSADM

For SSADM an external entity represents a source or recipient (or both) of information in a system. An external entity can be decomposed to sublevels if required, and it may also be replicated to make the data flow diagram more readable.

An external entity is graphically represented by an oval symbol which contains the name of the external entity. A replicated external entity contains a line at the top of the symbol with a lower-case alphabetic character to identify it, as in Figure 8.2. The name or identifier of a decomposed external entity is formed of its own name in addition to the identifier of the parent external entity and a numeric suffix, as shown in Figure 8.3.

PROCESS

A process represents an activity which transforms information from input to output

The definition is general as it covers update processes, which change the values of information, and report processes, which move information from one place to another, usually reformatting the way in which that information may be viewed.

For example, in Aquaduct, the process Close job proposal is an update process that transforms the information recorded about a job proposal to indicate that the job proposal is closed. The process Send balance and details to accountant is a report process which moves and reformats customer information and sends it to the accountant.

MEIN

For MEIN a process represents the transformation of the information input to an activity to the information output from the activity.

A process is an activity.

Figure 8.4 *Process Purchase from supplier (MEIN).*

Figure 8.5 *Primitive process Prepare purchase order (MEIN).*

A process is graphically represented by a circle that contains the name of the process and a number which serves as process identifier. An example is shown in Figure 8.4.

Where a process has been decomposed its process identifier contains the identifier of its parent process. A *primitive process* refers to a process represented on the lowest level DFD which cannot be decomposed further, as shown in Figure 8.5.

In Figure 8.5, the process contains its own identifier number ('2') in addition to the identifier ('2') of its parent process Purchase from supplier from Figure 8.4.

SSADM

In SSADM, a process represents an activity in the organisation that transforms information. A process is graphically represented by a rectangle divided into three parts which contain the process identifier, the name of the process and the location (the part of the organisation where the process is carried out, shown on a physical DFD only).

Figure 8.6 shows an example where the number '2' on the left-hand top side is the process identifier and Purchase from supplier is the name of the process.

As for MEIN, a decomposed process has a process identifier formed from the identifier of its parent process. An *elementary process* in SSADM is a process on the lowest level DFD that cannot be decomposed further, and it is indicated by an

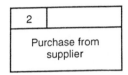

Figure 8.6   Process Purchase from supplier (SSADM).

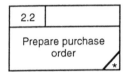

Figure 8.7   Elementary process Prepare purchase order with identifier (SSADM).

elementary process identifier, represented by an asterisk which is placed at the bottom of the right-hand side of the process symbol, as in Figure 8.7.

EVENT

> An event represents an important occurrence in a system or its environment which provides information or initiates a process

This concept is not provided in the MEIN or SSADM DFD.

DATA FLOW

> A data flow represents information input to or output from a process

A data flow represents the movement of information within a system or between a system and its environment. It can take many forms, which all share the characteristic that they are information-bearing. For example, an invoice, document, vocal message or electronic message. A data flow is allowed between processes, between a process and a data store (see below) and between a process and an external entity.

In the case study, for example, the information supplied by a customer when a job request is made is represented by a data flow between the customer and a

An event provides information or initiates a process.

process in the Aquaduct system. An internal example is the flow of information concerning the prices of parts when a job proposal is costed.

MEIN

For MEIN, a data flow represents the channel along which information is carried from one part of a system to another.

The graphical representation of a data flow is a line with an arrowhead showing the direction of the flow. The description of the data flow is written next to the line, as in Figure 8.8.

SSADM

For SSADM a data flow represents the information input to and output from a system, as well as the movement of information within the system. As for MEIN, a data flow is represented by a line, with an arrowhead showing the direction of the flow. The description of the data flow is written next to the line, as in Figure 8.9.

A data flow is information input to or output from a process.

DATA STORE

A data store represents a store of information input to or output from a process

A data store is like a file and it acts as a buffer to hold information that is required by processes.

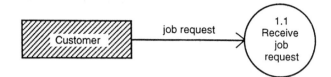

Figure 8.8   Data flow job request between external entity customer and Receive job request process (MEIN).

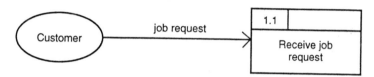

Figure 8.9   Data flow job request between external entity customer and Receive job request process (SSADM).

For example, in Aquaduct, information concerning customer and supplier accounts is stored in data stores.

MEIN

In MEIN, a data store represents an intermediate deposit or store of information used by processes. Creation or transformation of information does not take place within these stores, and they are only used as a temporary buffer or resting place for information until required by a process.

The graphical representation of a data store is two parallel lines with the data store name placed between them. An example is shown in Figure 8.10.

SSADM

In SSADM, a data store is used to represent a repository or store of information, such as a computer file or a card index.

SSADM defines two types of data store. The first is the *main* data store, which represents information held centrally and which is used by different processes. The second is the *transient* data store which represents information held temporarily, to be used by a process and then deleted.

A data store is a store of information input to or output from a process.

Customer
account

Figure 8.10 *Data store customer account (MEIN).*

The graphical representation of a data store is an open-ended rectangle containing its name. A data store has a reference number to identify it from other data stores. A capital letter 'D' is used to indicate a main data store and a transient data store is identified by a capital letter 'T'.

A data store can be decomposed into lower levels. Its reference number contains the reference number of the parent data store.

Data stores which are replicated on a diagram are shown by a double line at the closed end of the rectangle. Figure 8.11 shows an example of replicated and decomposed data stores.

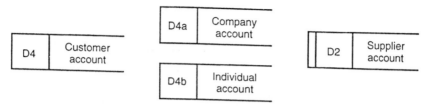

Figure 8.11 Decomposed data store customer account into company account and individual account data stores; replicated data store supplier account (SSADM).

Figure 8.12 Data store purchase order used by one process only (SSADM).

In SSADM there are also data stores used by only one elementary process; in this case, the reference number of the data store may contain the reference number of the process, as seen in Figure 8.12.

SUMMARY

We have presented a comparison of the process modelling concepts of the DFD models for MEIN and SSADM, and Table 8.1 shows how the methods compare for these concepts.

Table 8.1 Process modelling concepts in MEIN and SSADM data flow diagram

Concept	MEIN	Term	SSADM	Term
External entity	yes	external entity	yes	external entity (replicated and decomposed)
Process	yes	process primitive process	yes	process elementary process
Event	–		–	
Data flow	yes	data flow	yes	data flow
Data store	yes	data store	yes	data store (decomposed and replicated)

Table 8.2 Graphical representation of process modelling concepts in MEIN and SSADM data flow diagram

Concept	MEIN	SSADM
External entity	Customer	a Customer a1 Company decomposed replicated external entity
Process	2 Purchase from supplier	2 | Purchases Purchase from supplier
Event	not represented	not represented
Data flow	job request $E \longrightarrow P$	job request $E \longrightarrow P$
Data store	Customer account	D4 | Customer account D4a | Company account decomposed data store D2 | Supplier account replicated data store

Correspondences

Table 8.1 shows that the basic concepts in the methods are equivalent.

Minor differences

Some differences between MEIN and SSADM in the modelling of detail are:

1. SSADM has replicated and decomposed external entities and data stores.
2. SSADM provides an elementary process identifier, showing the lowest level of process.

   The surface differences in the graphical representations of the DFD concepts are shown in Table 8.2.

CONCLUSIONS

Reference framework concepts

MEIN and SSADM correspond for all concepts considered, and graphical representations are very similar. An important concept which is not provided in either DFD is the event.

Method scope

SSADM provides the facility to decompose data stores and external entities, providing more control of graphical detail.

Chapter 9

CASE STUDY – DISCUSSION AND PROCESS MODEL SOLUTION IN SSADM AND MEIN

This chapter consists of two sections:

I. In the first section, detailed comments are made on a range of topics which will assist the student to understand the case study and its DFD-based process model solution.

II. In the second section, the process model solution is presented in SSADM and MEIN. This consists of (a) annotated case study text for requirements tracing, (b) DFD process models, (c) data dictionary.

I. COMMENTS ON CASE STUDY SOLUTION

In this section we discuss several topics which cover general issues in building DFD-based process models, as well as making comments on various aspects of the specific models presented in Section II.

The topics covered are:

- general principles for building DFD-based process models;

- structure of SSADM and MEIN DFD;

- how to build a DFD in practice;

- general rules for building data stores from structure models;

- specific principles for mapping structure model objects to data stores in this case study;

- comments on the case study structure model mapping to the data dictionary;

- guide to process and data flow in the DFD;

- case study omissions and ambiguities.

GENERAL PRINCIPLES FOR BUILDING DFD-BASED PROCESS MODELS

Aim of DFD-based process model

As for structure modelling, the aim of the process model may be user-centred or developer-centred. For a DFD-based model, the user-centred aim focuses on the flow of processes, with data being of secondary importance. The reason for this is that, in validation, the user is mainly interested in the correspondence between the activities performed in the organisation and the processes on the DFD.

In contrast, a developer-centred aim might emphasise the efficiency of data representation and access in data stores.

As we are aiming for high graphical visibility and understandability of the graphical process model, the user-centred aim is adopted throughout the case study process model.

Form of DFD-based process model

This usually consists of two main parts: the DFD and the data dictionary. The textual data dictionary defines the detail of the data items in the data stores and flows shown on the graphical DFD. It may also describe the external entities.

Integration of structure and process models

For the Aquaduct case study, a structure model has been built as shown in Chapter 6, and to save redoing development work and to avoid inconsistency, we need to integrate this with the process model. As the structure model has identified the objects about which information is to be recorded, integration is achieved by defining data stores in the DFD that correspond to structure model objects.

The structure model serves directly as the basis for the data dictionary but is also of indirect use, as we shall see below, when identifying processes.

STRUCTURE OF MEIN AND SSADM DFD

MEIN

MEIN employs a technique termed explosion, which decomposes a process of a DFD into a lower level DFD with more processes, and so on until the required level of detail is reached.

An exploded DFD consists of:

- A *context diagram* which represents a system and its boundary. In the diagram, the system is represented as a single process with the system name. External entities are connected by data flows to and from the system.

- An *intermediate level data flow diagram* which is obtained when the context diagram is exploded, showing processes, data stores, data flows and external entities. Further intermediate level data flow diagrams are obtained by exploding the processes of this diagram and so on until the primitive processes are reached.

SSADM

In SSADM, process decomposition is termed *levelling*, which allows the decomposition of a complex process as many times as necessary until the required level of detail is reached.

A levelled DFD consists of:

- A *context diagram* or *level 0 diagram*, whose purpose is to show a general view of the system. Only one process with the name of the system is shown, as well as the main data flows to and from the external entities.

- A *level 1 diagram* or *top level diagram*, which shows the main processes together with the external entities, data stores and data flows.

- Lower-level diagrams (level 2, level 3 to level *N*) which are the result of decomposing processes from higher-level diagrams.

HOW TO BUILD A DFD IN PRACTICE

Processes

We suggest that you begin by identifying processes. Some guidelines for identifying these are as follows, and they assume that a structure model is available:

- From the requirements text, locate the entities and relationships from the structure model and identify the processes that operate on these objects.

- Group the processes into main application areas that are of interest to the user.

- Decompose these application areas into processes and process groupings. The criteria for process groupings may vary between different information systems, but attempt to group processes in a way that is familiar to users. For example, you can group processes into those involved in the same data flows.

Data stores and flows

Data stores are determined next and are based on the structure model. Data stores are stores that are local for processes, and, having identified these, they will determine the data flows between stores and processes that exist. Data store building guidelines are discussed below.

External entities

External entities were defined in Chapter 8 as representing information sources or destinations about which information is not to be recorded. However, it is very common for many external entities to represent objects about which information is recorded, such as customer and supplier shown in Figure 9.2. Those that do not have information recorded are, for example job costing and accountant.

On the other hand, it may be argued that an external entity, for example customer, which inputs data to a process, does not actually represent a customer, but instead represents an agent (about which we do not wish to record information) associated with the customer.

Once external entities have been defined, then the flows between these and processes may be defined.

GENERAL RULES FOR BUILDING DATA STORES FROM STRUCTURE MODELS

The structure model objects that are required to be mapped to data stores are entity, attribute and relationship. Here we give some first level mapping rules that may be applied in any situation:

- An attribute is mapped into a data item which is in the same data store as the entity to which the attribute is related.

- An entity should not be split over data stores. It should be mapped to either:
  - a data store containing just one entity (a 1:1 entity-data store mapping)
  - a data store containing other entities (an N:1 entity-data store mapping)

- A relationship between entities A and B may be mapped to the data store(s) of either (a) entity A, (b) entity B or (c) both entities.

SPECIFIC PRINCIPLES FOR MAPPING STRUCTURE MODEL OBJECTS TO DATA STORES IN THIS CASE STUDY

Entities and data stores

The main consideration is how the entities in the structure model are to be mapped to data stores, as the general principles above are not specific enough.

If each entity is mapped to a single data store, then there will usually be many data stores and consequently there will be too many data flows on the DFD. This type of mapping regards each data store as important as any other. On the other hand, if many entities are mapped to only a small number of data stores, there will be too few stores, important entities may be lost in detail and the data flow descriptions will be complex.

We want to introduce a level of detail so that some entities are more important than others and hence more visible, and we do this by mapping important entities into data stores and naming the data stores after these entities, and mapping less important entities into the data stores corresponding to the important entities.

The criteria we use for deciding which entities are more important than others usually depend on user perception and will vary between information systems. In the absence of a user for this case study, we have used a combination of three factors:

1. number of processes – are there many different processes which operate on a given entity?

2. processing phase – does this entity mark a significant processing phase, in the overall processing sequence?

3. number of relationships – does this entity have only a few relationships?

It should be noted that these factors are subjective and may be applied with different results. We emphasise that, in practice, the user should be involved in these important decisions.

The main reason for the principle of level of detail is that, following our user-centred aim, data stores are subordinate to processes in a DFD. The main aim of a DFD is to show the flow of data from one process to another, and data stores should be chosen so that this kind of process flow is as visible as possible.

Relationships

Relationship mappings

Three ways of mapping an entity relationship R(AB) to data stores are now described.

Entities in same data store
Where entities A and B are mapped to the same data store their relationship does not need to be represented further. This often applies to 1:1 relationships and 1:N relationships where entity B 'belongs' to entity A; for example, customer payment and customer.

Entities in different data store – relevant data items duplicated
The relevant data items for entity A (from its data store) are included in the data store for entity B. For example, in the case study, to represent the job request:customer relationship (with the meaning of the customer who originated this job request) the relevant customer data items from data store D4 are included in the job request data store D5, as shown in the data dictionary in Section II.

Entities in different data store – identifier represents relationship
Only the identifier of entity A is included in the data store for entity B. For example, for the purchase order:supplier relationship in data store D6, only the supplier number identifier of supplier is used to represent the relationship.

Where such a relationship is used, as in process 3.3.1 in Figure 9.8, then the data store D2 is also required by the process, so that the relevant supplier data items can be obtained from D2 once the identifier is obtained from D6.

Relationship constraints

In our data dictionary, relationship constraints are not explicitly represented in the data stores. You should be aware when you are defining processes that use a data store whether that data store contains 'repeating groups'. For example, data store D4 contains a repeating group of customer payments for each customer represented in the store. Some data dictionaries indicate relationship constraints with different types of brackets, for example showing the above repeating group as {customer payment}. Optional data items may also be indicated.

Efficiency of data stores

As we are not on the logical design level and we are building a user-centred model, then the efficiency of the data item content of the stores is not a consideration. In particular, you should note that we regard the normalisation technique often applied to data stores as belonging on the logical design level. There are several areas to consider:

Structure

We do not specify how relationships are represented within a data store or which data items are related. We are also not concerned with questions of efficient access to any individual data item in the stores, or how a given data item may be located in a data store containing many different items.

Duplication

Duplication is common in data stores, for example in data store D5, where customer data items, representing the job request:customer relationship, are duplicates of those in data store D4.

Duplication allows us to avoid many data stores and flows around a process, as all relevant information can be held in one (or few) data stores.

Process integration

The purpose of data stores on the DFD is to provide data items for processes. When mapping objects to data stores you should obviously ensure that all the data items required by any processes that use that data store are present. Where a relationship is represented only by an identifier, then the related data store should be available for that process also.

COMMENTS ON THE CASE STUDY STRUCTURE MODEL MAPPING TO THE DATA DICTIONARY

Entities and data stores

Six data stores have been modelled based on 24 entities in the structure model. Parts (D1), job proposal and job order (D3), customer account (D4) and supplier account (D2) all have several different processes that operate on them. Purchase order (D6) is somewhat solitary, and job request (D5) marks a significant processing phase, as this was the possible start of a job order. The data dictionary shows which entities have been mapped to which data stores. All attributes have 'followed' their entity.

Relationships and data stores

The data dictionary shows which relationships have been mapped to which data stores.

Entities in same data store

1:N relationship
For customer account:customer payment, or supplier account:bill, the relationship between the entities is represented by the fact that the entities are in the same data store (data stores D4 and D2 respectively). Manager:job order is another example found in data store D3 and part:supply is found in data store D1.

1:1 relationship
For project:initiative and project:advertising campaign the entities are stored in data store D3.

Entities in different data store - identifier represents relationship

N:1 relationship
Purchase order:supplier is represented by the supplier number data item (supplier identifier) in data store D6.

M:N relationship

Part:job order is represented twice, in both D1 and D3 data stores (to which part and job order entities are mapped respectively), using the joint identifiers (job order number and part number) of part and job order. The information concerning the relationship is thus available for processes which use either data store.

Job proposal:part relationship is represented once in data store D3.

Entities in different data store – relevant data items duplicated

Job request:customer is represented by including the relevant customer information in the D5 data store.

Additional data items

The detailed step of process modelling often brings about the realisation that additional data items are required. For example, it has been decided to model the states of the entities job request, job order and job proposal, so that information is recorded concerning the different states in which these objects may exist. A job proposal may be, for example, either 'prepared', 'accepted' or 'rejected'. The condition data item in the relevant data store is set to these values.

GUIDE TO PROCESS AND DATA FLOW IN THE DFD

This discussion is a 'walkthrough' with the DFDs in Section II and describes the processing and the data they use, emphasising the data from and to data stores. In this way you can see where the data required by each process is located. The discussion also explains the nature of the data existing in the different data flows.

Process 1 Proposal elaborating

Process 1.1 – receives a request for a job from a customer and decides to accept or reject the request.

The request is checked in by making an entry on the D5 data store. The entry consists of job request attributes and the customer details shown in D5. If it is accepted the job request is scheduled for later attention. If rejected, a rejection letter is sent to the customer.

Process 1.2 – obtains information concerning a job request and prepares a job proposal and job order.

All information concerning a job request (including customer information) is obtained from D5 and the parts and labour required are extracted from the description data item. A labour list is sent to the job costing section who provide the labour cost, and the prices for the parts are obtained from the D1 data store. Labour cost and part prices are then included in an entry for job proposal and job order data items which is made on the D3 data store.

The customer number for this job proposal is recorded and the part numbers for the job proposal and order.

Process 1.3 – receives job order and job proposal information from process 1.2 and sends the information on forms to the customer for approval.

Process 1.4 – the customer sends back a rejection for the proposal and an entry is made on D3 setting the condition data item of job proposal to rejected.

Process 1.5 – the customer sends the first payment and the job order, which should be signed. Information is obtained from D3 concerning the job order and the entry in D3 concerning job order is updated with condition set to either signed or not signed.

Process 1.6 – receives customer, job order and payment information from process 1.5 and updates the D4 data store balance data item in the account.

Process 1.7 – receives customer information from process 1.6 and sends a receipt and the proposal to the customer.

Process 2   Purchase from supplier

Process 2.1 – obtains the parts required for a job order from the job order:part information on D3 and checks they are in stock by examining the quantity and stock data items on the relevant entries in D1.

Process 2.2 – for those parts not in stock, purchase orders are prepared. Information on supplier numbers of parts, and parts details, is obtained from D1 and information concerning supplier names and addresses is obtained from D2. Entries are made on D6 representing purchase orders, including the purchase order:part relationship.

Process 2.3 – purchase order information is received from process 2.2 and is included on purchase order forms which are sent to suppliers.

Process 2.4 – parts are assigned to their job order by updating the entries in D1 concerning the job order number data item. Parts information is received from both process 2.1 and process 2.5.

Process 2.5 – bills and receipts for parts supplied by suppliers are received.

Process 2.6 – bill and receipt information is received from process 2.5 and updates made to entries in D2 concerning balance, bill and receipt.

Process 3.1 Customer accounting

Process 3.1.1 – the customer sends in a payment which is checked using account information obtained from D4.

Process 3.1.2 – payment details are received from process 3.1.1 and the balance and customer payment items are updated in D4.

Process 3.1.3 – every month the customer accounts are checked, looking at the balance data item from D4.

Process 3.1.4 – an end-of-job report is prepared based on information received from process 3.1.3 concerning finished job order numbers. Information concerning parts and prices for any completed job orders is obtained from D1 (using part number/job order number). The customer account items on D4 are set to reflect end of job.

Process 3.1.5 – using customer information received from process 3.1.3, customer reminder information is prepared and a customer reminder entry made in D4.

Process 3.1.6 – the end-of-job report from process 3.1.4 is sent to the customer.

Process 3.1.7 – the customer reminder from process 3.1.5 is sent to the customer.

Process 3.1.8 – using customer information received from process 3.1.4 account details are obtained from D4.

Process 3.1.9 – account details from process 3.1.8 are sent to the accountant.

Process 3.2 Supplier accounting

Process 3.2.1 – on receiving a reminder from a supplier the account is checked by obtaining information from D2. The supplier reminder items are updated and the amount checked.

Process 3.2.2 – the amount of the reminder is paid by updating the supplier payment data items in D2 and sending the payment to the supplier.

Process 3.2.3 – if the reminder amount was inconsistent with the account balance, supplier information is received from process 3.2.1, and account details are obtained from D2.

Process 3.2.4 – receiving supplier account details from process 3.2.3 these are sent to the accountant.

Process 3.3   Reporting part transactions

Process 3.3.1 – every month, information concerning parts used by job orders, purchase orders and which parts have been supplied by which suppliers is required. This is obtained from the D1 and D6 data stores, using the purchase order number/part number, supplier number, and part number/job order number data items, and the D2 data store, using the supplier data items.

Process 3.3.2 – information from process 3.3.1 is received and included in a report to be sent to the accountant.

CASE STUDY OMISSIONS AND AMBIGUITIES

Reduction of case study complexity

As for the structure model case study solution, some elements have been omitted from the process model to reduce the complexity of the solution. In a real situation, it is often not clear whether a process description is 'context' or not; that is, whether it is intended to be performed within the system with which we are concerned or a related system. In cases such as these, further information must be obtained from the user.

Omissions

Data stores

- Data concerning the following entities from the entity–attribute list is not used in data stores (and no processes reference them): complaint, department, section, employee and security guard.

- The following entities have been mapped to data stores but are not referenced by any process. Suggestions are made as to how they might be used if the process model was expanded:
    Salesperson (D4) – created when a customer account is set up.
    Manager (D3) – created when a job order is set up.
    Presentation (D3) – set up at any time (optional).
    Project (D3) – set up at any time (optional).
    Initiative (D3) – set up at any time (optional).
    Advertising campaign (D3) – set up at any time (optional).

Process

- Complaints and presentation processes are not modelled (paragraphs 4 and 5).

- The process to record the date and time for a supplier and part is not modelled (paragraph 8).

- The iterative process for the parts transactions report is not modelled (paragraph 12). Alternatively, this might be a lower-level process of process 3.3.1.
- Part quality processes are not modelled (paragraph 12).

Ambiguities

There are several important.facts which are not supplied by the case study but which would be needed to proceed to a design stage. It is necessary to know how and when details for the customer, supplier, part and supplier entities are created. At present, the model assumes that entity instances already exist.

Additional points

The job proposal:part relationship exists in data store D3 (it is created by process 1.2) but no process uses this information. The relationship may be redundant and hence may be removed from the structure model.

This is a good example of how information from process modelling may be used to improve the structure model.

II. CASE STUDY SOLUTION – PROCESS MODEL IN SSADM AND MEIN

This section presents the DFD-based process model solution for the case study. The solution is in three parts:

1. The case study text from Chapter 1 is repeated with the addition of detail to make requirements tracing between the text and the process model easier. We do this by listing, under each numbered text paragraph, the names and numbers of the processes which are introduced in that paragraph. These may then be related to the processes on the DFD.

   In addition, items in data stores in the data dictionary are annotated with the numbers of the DFD processes which read or write that data item.

2. The DFDs for SSADM and MEIN.

3. A data dictionary, which includes: (a) data stores and their data item contents, (b) brief external entity descriptions. The methods do not suggest a precise form for the data dictionary, and they variously refer to concepts such as a data dictionary, encyclopaedia and data inventory. For this reason, as well as to avoid detailed repetition, just one list is provided for both the methods.

CASE STUDY TEXT

The case study from Chapter 1 is given below, listing the processes to be found in each paragraph.

Aquaduct plumber case study

(1) Potential or existing customers contact Aquaduct with their needs and, after ascertaining customer details, a job proposal is sent to them. On customer acceptance the proposal, or an amended version, becomes a job order, and a manager is assigned to the job order. Some job orders have several customers and a set of related job orders may be classed as a project.

> **Processes:** Receive job request (1.1), Prepare job order and job proposal (1.2), Send job order and job proposal to customer (1.3)

(2) There are several types of employee, including managers, salespersons and security guards. Employee details including card number, names, address and

telephone numbers are recorded; card number is unique and is mandatory, while the other details are optional; telephones are shared and several employees may have the same address. In addition, managers have a parking place number and salespeople have a sales club number. Security guards may be assigned to both buildings and car parks, but salespersons may be either telephone or direct salespersons. Customers are assigned to exactly two salespersons and employees work with other employees in teams.

Processes: none

(3) A customer holds an Aquaduct account for each relevant job order; the account belongs to the customer. Certain projects are very prestigious and the marketing department may plan an advertising campaign which publicises that project and the involvement of Aquaduct. Alternatively, a project may be publicised by sponsoring a local initiative, such as a school project or artistic festival, but it may not be publicised by both a campaign and an initiative. A campaign or initiative concern only one project and vice versa.

Processes: none

(4) A customer may be dissatisfied, as happens from time to time, and Aquaduct are proud of their complaints procedure which they set up to deal with this situation. This is described in the literature which is sent to every customer concerning a job order and involves a hot line telephone number for customers to phone. Complaints information recorded concerns the customer, the job order and the department concerned. Departments comprise sections and section names are unique only within their department.

Processes: none

(5) Apart from the benefit to customer relations provided by this procedure, Aquaduct find that complaints constitute a source of information that is useful for inducting new staff, as well as leading to reviews of organisation procedures. Information is recorded concerning presentations which may be made where managers talk about the experience of job orders with different customers. A manager can make a presentation about only one job order and one customer.

Processes: none

The activities that are carried out at the beginning and end of a job order, and those activities concerning payments, may be summarised as follows:

(6) *Job request.* Customers make job requests to Aquaduct, and in response the request may be rejected, or a job proposal may be written and sent to the

customers. The customer may approve or reject the proposal. If it is rejected the proposal is closed.

> **Processes:** Receive job request (1.1), Prepare job order and job proposal (1.2), Send job order and job proposal to customer (1.3), Close job proposal (1.4)

(7) *Job proposal.* A job proposal must specify the parts needed, their prices and the cost of labour, obtained from the job costing section. The proposal is sent to the customer with a job order form. If the customer approves the proposal, the customer must sign the job order form and make the first payment for the job order. Aquaduct sends the proposal and a receipt for the first payment to the customer.

> **Processes:** Prepare job order and job proposal (1.2), Send job order and job proposal to customer (1.3), Receive job order and 1st payment (1.5), Send proposal and 1st payment receipt (1.7)

(8) *Job order.* When the job order is signed, the file of parts is checked. If parts are not in stock, indicated by the quantities, a purchase order is prepared and sent to an approved supplier. The date and time when a supplier was approved for a part is recorded. The supplier must supply bills and receipts for any supplied parts, which are used to update the supplier account. A supplier should have an account eventually, but not necessarily initially. The parts file is updated with any new parts.

> **Processes:** Check stock (2.1), Prepare purchase order (2.2), Send purchase order to supplier (2.3), Receive bill and receipt (2.5), Update supplier account (2.6), Record parts (2.4)

(9) *Customer account.* When a job order is signed, the customer account is updated with customer details. At the end of the month a reminder is sent to a customer to pay a certain amount. On receipt of payment, the payment is checked against the customer account, which is then updated.

> **Processes:** Record customer details (1.6), Check customer account monthly (3.1.3), Prepare reminder (3.1.5), Send reminder to customer (3.1.7), Check payment (3.1.1), Update customer account (3.1.2)

(10) When a job has finished and the customer has made all the payments, an end-of-job report will be sent to the customer. In addition, the account balance is elaborated and sent, along with customer details, to the accountant.

> **Processes:** Check customer account monthly (3.1.3), Prepare end of job report (3.1.4), Send end of job report to customer (3.1.6),

Elaborate customer balance (3.1.8), Send balance and details to accountant (3.1.9)

(11) *Supplier account.* The suppliers should send reminders every end of month to Aquaduct. Aquaduct checks the supplier account and, if valid, makes a payment to the supplier. The supplier account is updated. If the reminder amount is inconsistent with the supplier account, then the supplier account balance is elaborated and sent, along with supplier details, to the accountant.

Processes: Check supplier account (3.2.1), Make payment (3.2.2), Elaborate supplier balance (3.2.3), Send balance and details to accountant (3.2.4)

(12) *Parts file.* At the end of every month, a report about transactions on parts is produced and sent to the accountant. If an error exists in the report it is redone. To monitor part quality, information may be kept for each part supplied by a supplier, recording ratings and the date of the ratings.

Processes: Produce report on transactions (3.3.1), Send report to accountant (3.3.2)

DATA FLOW DIAGRAMS

Figures 9.1 to 9.16 show the DFDs for SSADM and MEIN for the case study.

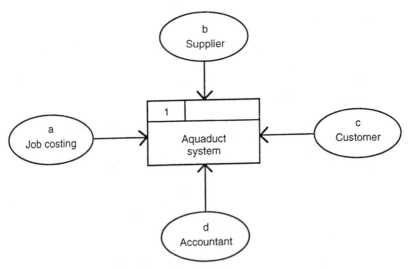

Figure 9.1 *Aquaduct system context diagram (SSADM).*

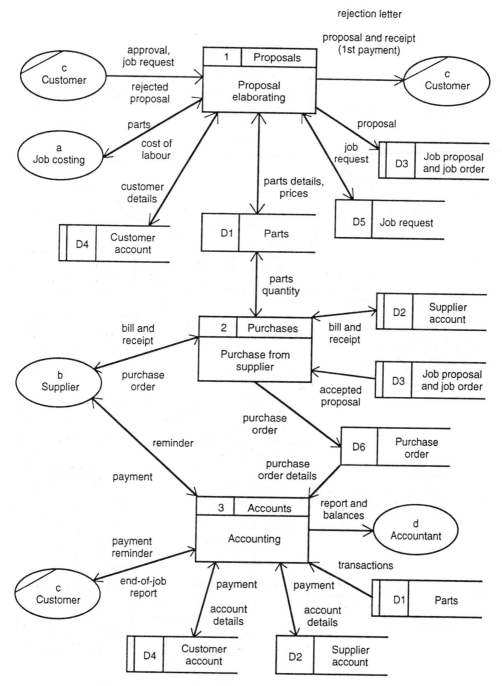

Figure 9.2 Top-level current logical data flow diagram (SSADM).

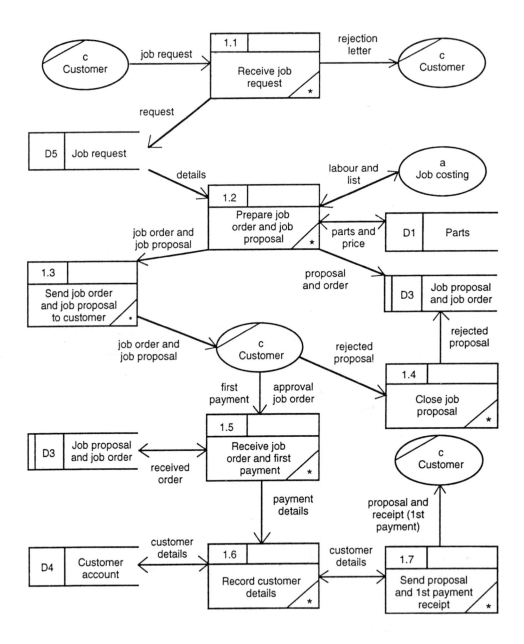

Figure 9.3 Sublevel process number 1 Proposal elaborating (SSADM).

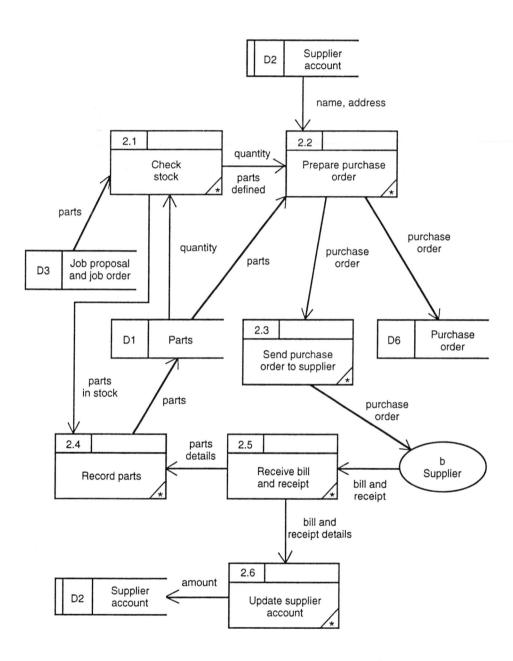

Figure 9.4 Sublevel process number 2 Purchase from supplier (SSADM).

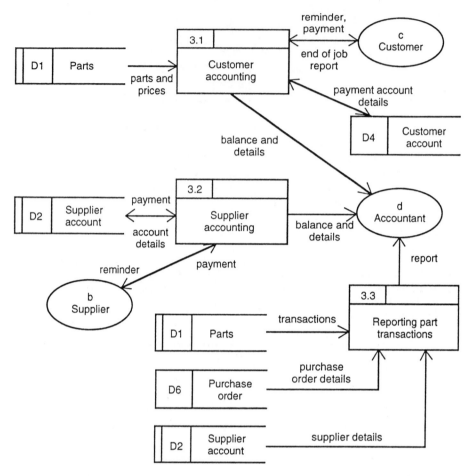

Figure 9.5 Sublevel process 3 Accounting (SSADM).

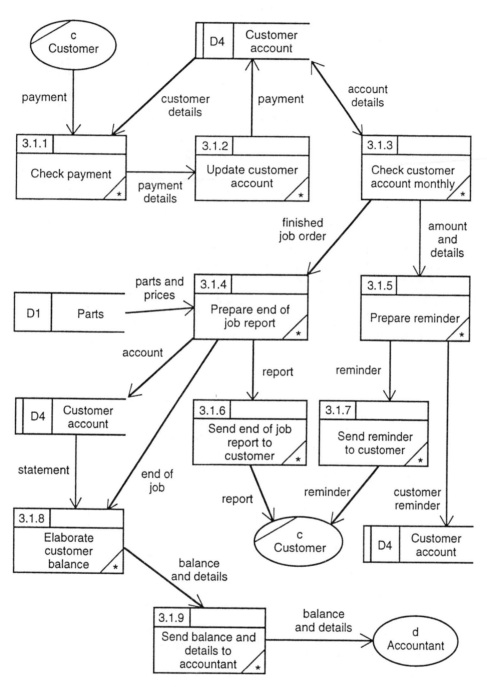

Figure 9.6 Sublevel process number 3.1 Customer accounting (SSADM).

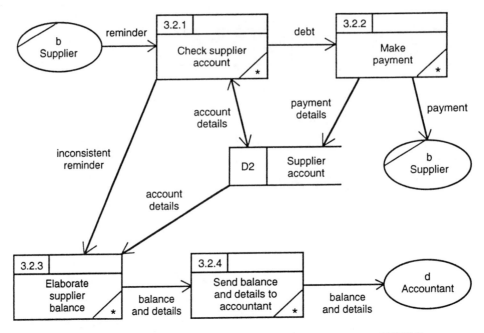

Figure 9.7 Sublevel process number 3.2 Supplier accounting (SSADM).

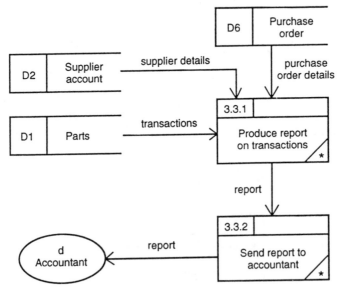

Figure 9.8 Sublevel process number 3.3 Reporting part transactions (SSADM).

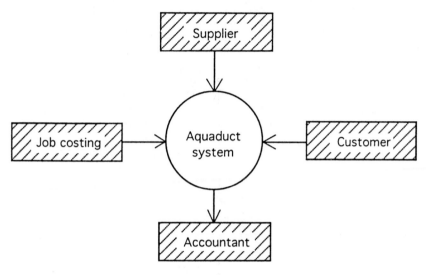

Figure 9.9   Aquaduct system context diagram (MEIN).

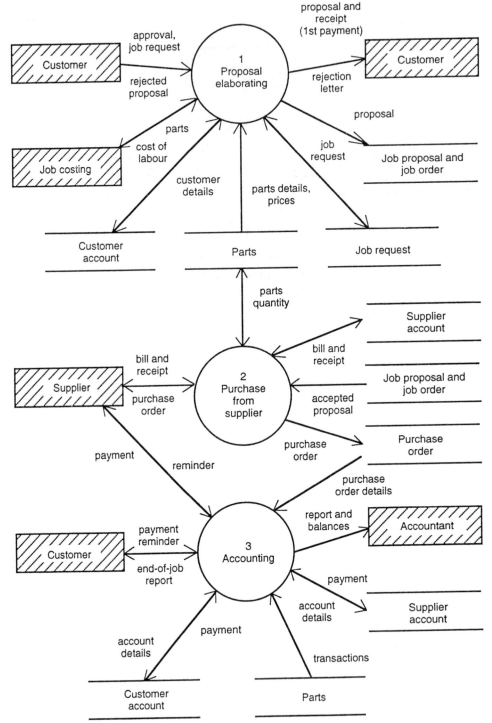

Figure 9.10 Top-level current logical data flow diagram (MEIN).

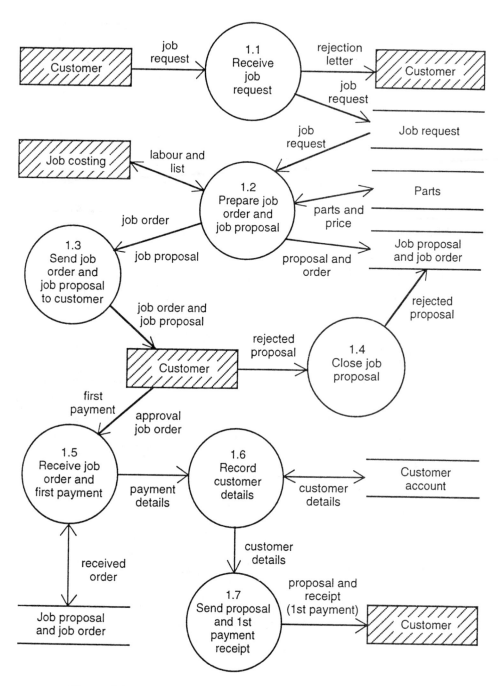

Figure 9.11   Sublevel process number 1 Proposal elaborating (MEIN).

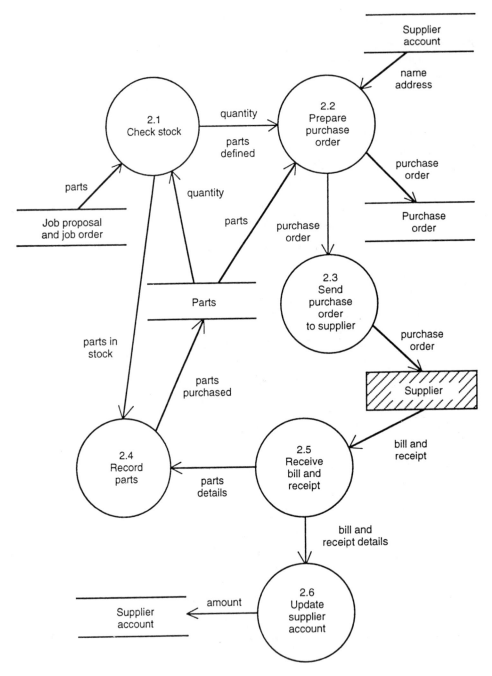

Figure 9.12 Sublevel process number 2 Purchase from supplier (MEIN).

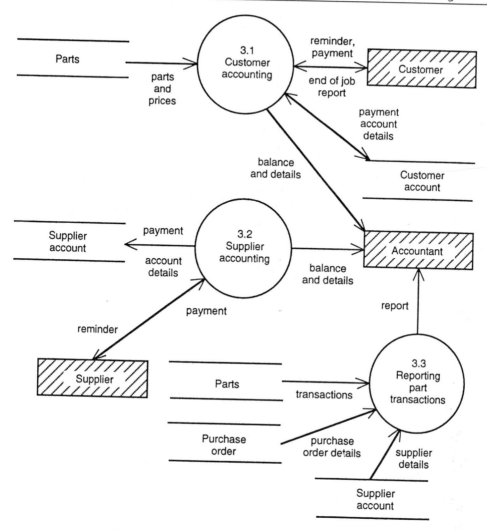

Figure 9.13 Sublevel process 3 Accounting (MEIN).

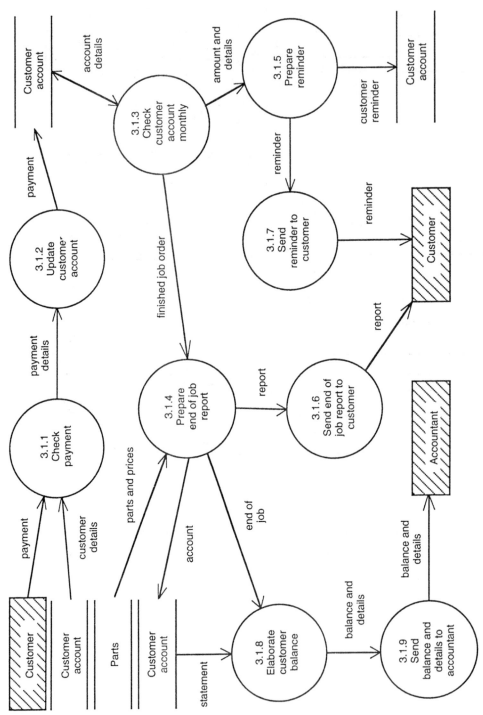

Figure 9.14 Sublevel process number 3.1 Customer accounting (MEIN).

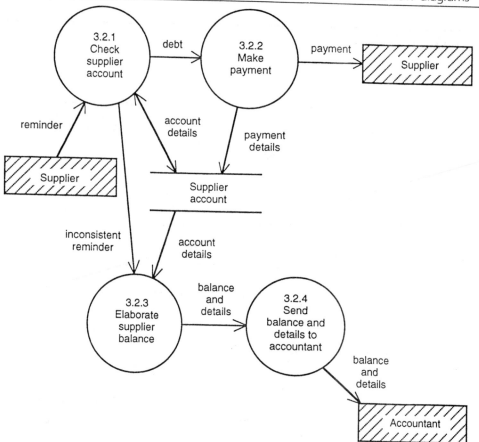

Figure 9.15   Sublevel process number 3.2 Supplier accounting (MEIN).

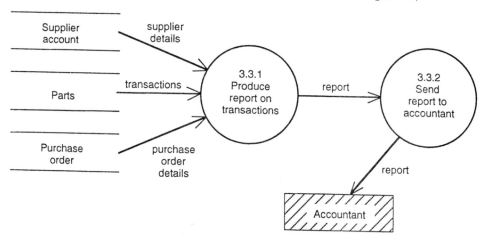

Figure 9.16   Sublevel process number 3.3 Reporting part transactions (MEIN).

DATA DICTIONARY

Data stores

Name	Entity/ Relationship	Data items	DFD process (R – read; W – write)
D1 Parts	part	part number price quantity stock	1.2R, 2.1R, 2.2R
	supply	supplier number/part number date time quality (rating, date)	2.2R
	part:job order	part number/job order number date price	2.4W, 3.1.4R, 3.3.1R
D2 Supplier account	supplier	supplier number name address telephone number	2.2R, 3.2.1R, 3.2.3R
	supplier account	supplier account number credit limit balance	2.6W
	bill	bill number part number amount date	2.6W
	receipt	receipt number part number amount date	2.6W
	supplier reminder	supplier reminder number date amount	3.2.1W
	supplier payment	supplier payment number amount date	3.2.1W

Name	Entity/ Relationship	Data items	DFD process (R – read; W – write)
D3 Job proposal and job order	job proposal	job proposal number labour cost parts cost description date condition	
	job order	job order number description budget date condition	1.2W, 1.4W
	manager	card number name address telephone number parking place number	1.2W, 1.5R, 1.5W
	presentation	customer number/ job order number/card number date time	
	project	project number date	
	initiative	initiative name	
	advertising campaign	name budget agency name date	
	job proposal:part	job proposal number/part number	
	job proposal: customer	job proposal number/ customer number	1.2W
	job order:part	job order number/part number	1.2W, 1.5R
D4 Customer account	customer	customer number name address telephone number	1.2W, 2.1R
	customer account	customer number/job order number credit limit balance	3.1.8R
			1.6W, 3.1.1R, 3.1.2W, 3.1.4W, 3.1.3R

Name	Entity/ Relationship	Data items	DFD process (R – read; W – write)
	salesperson	card number name address telephone number sales club number	
	customer payment	payment number amount date	3.1.2W
	customer reminder	reminder number date amount	3.1.5W
D5 Job request	job request	job request number date description condition	1.1W, 1.2R
	job request: customer	customer number name address telephone number	1.1W, 1.2R
D6 Purchase order	purchase order	purchase order number amount date	2.2W
	purchase order: supplier	supplier number	
	purchase order:part	purchase order number/ part number	2.2W, 3.3.1R

External entities

- *Accountant*. Financial and budgeting part of Aquaduct not included in the case study

- *Customer*. An individual or part of an external organisation, who wish Aquaduct to perform a service for them, who send data to or receive data from Aquaduct

- *Job costing*. Section of Aquaduct who calculate labour costs. Not included in the case study application

- *Supplier.* An individual or part of an external organisation, who supply Aquaduct with parts, who send data to or receive data from Aquaduct.

Data flows

Although often included in the data dictionary, the data flows are described earlier with their related processes under the heading 'Guide to process and data flow in the DFD' to make their meaning clearer.

Chapter 10

PROCESS MODELS WITH CONTROL STRUCTURES

INTRODUCTION

This chapter describes process modelling in Information Engineering (IE), MERISE and the Entity Life History (ELH) technique of SSADM, all of which represent control structures in their process models. We briefly describe the types of diagrams in the methods and then the reference framework concepts and viewpoints we use for the comparison.

PROCESS MODELLING DIAGRAM TYPES

IE

In IE, process modelling may be expressed in the process decomposition, process dependency and process data flow diagrams. The process decomposition diagram is used to decompose system processes into lower-level processes until the level of required detail is reached.

The process dependency diagram incorporates control structure and shows how the processes in the process decomposition diagram are interrelated. Finally, the process data flow diagram is a type of DFD which is an extension to a process dependency diagram, showing the information input to and output from the processes in the system, and describing the fundamental interactions that are necessary among the processes (Martin 1990).

The diagrams are usually related such that one dependency or data flow diagram may be an elaboration of one process from the decomposition diagram.

MERISE

MERISE uses two types of diagram for process modelling, the flow diagram (FD) and the conceptual processing model (CPM). The flow diagram is a very high-level one-page diagram, similar to a DFD context diagram, that is used to represent the flows of information between different external entities and the system.

A CPM shows a major process and its data flows for a given area of the system, without taking into account the 'how', 'who', 'when' and 'where' (Quang and Chartier-Kastler 1991), and is made up of operations which may be broken down into lower-level tasks. A system is thus typically modelled by many CPMs.

REFERENCE FRAMEWORK

Concepts

The concepts we consider are those defined in Chapter 8 with the addition of the control structure concept. We shall also rely upon the definitions introduced in that chapter. The concepts are: external entity, process, event, data flow, data store and control structure.

Viewpoints

We define the notion of viewpoint in this chapter, and discuss the different viewpoints provided by the method diagrams.

EXTERNAL ENTITY

IE

IE does not represent external entities.

MERISE

In MERISE, an external entity is termed an *actor*, which is an agent able to exchange information with another actors (Quang and Chartier-Kastler 1991), and it may be internal or external.

An external actor exists outside the boundary of the system and of the organisation, while an internal actor exists outside of the boundary of the system, but within the organisation. An actor is a basic component of the flow diagram, and it can be a person, organisation or another system. Detailed information concerned with internal or external actors is not intended to be recorded.

An actor is graphically represented by an oval shape within which its name is written. To distinguish between internal and external actors, a dark background pattern for external actors is used, as shown in Figure 10.1.

Figure 10.1 *Internal and external actors accountant and customer (MERISE).*

PROCESS

IE

A *process* in IE represents a specific activity that has a definable beginning and ending and has identifiable inputs and outputs (Martin 1990). A process may be triggered by an event (see below) or by another process. It is graphically represented by a soft box within which its name is written, as in Figure 10.2.

The decomposition of a process may be shown on a process dependency diagram, where decomposed processes are shown within a large process box. At the top of the box, a line is drawn above which the name of the expanded process is written. Figure 10.3 shows a process dependency diagram for the decomposed process of Figure 10.2. Other symbols will be explained later.

IE uses the term *elementary process* to refer to a process which cannot be decomposed further. Such processes are the bottom nodes of the process decomposition and process dependency diagrams.

An elementary process is defined as 'the smallest unit of activity of meaning to the end user, and which when complete leaves the information area in a self consistent state' (Martin 1990). Figure 10.4 shows, on the lowest level, the elementary processes which are the decomposition of the high-level process Reporting part transactions.

IE uses three dots to graphically indicate that a process is not elementary and can be expanded into more detail. The three dots are set at the right-hand top side of the process box which can be expanded. An example is shown in Figure 10.5.

MERISE

MERISE uses three terms which refer to different levels of a process: *process*, *operation* and *task*. The terms are hierarchically related, as one or more tasks comprise an operation and one or more operations comprise a process.

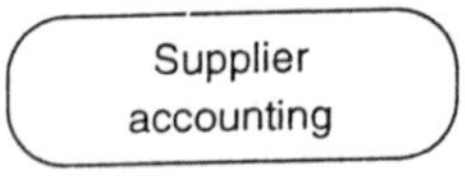

Supplier
accounting

Figure 10.2 *Process Supplier accounting (IE).*

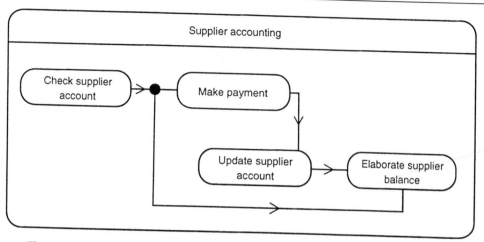

Figure 10.3   Exploded process Supplier accounting showing a process dependency diagram (IE).

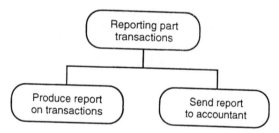

Figure 10.4   Decomposition diagram showing elementary processes (IE).

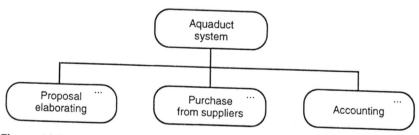

Figure 10.5   Processes with expansion indicator are processes that can be further decomposed (IE).

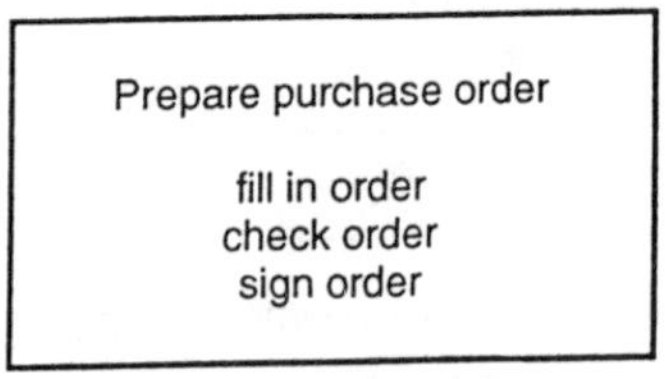

```
┌─────────────────────────────┐
│     Prepare purchase order  │
│                             │
│          fill in order      │
│          check order        │
│          sign order         │
└─────────────────────────────┘
```

Figure 10.6 *Operation Prepare purchase order with tasks (MERISE).*

Process

A process represents an area of activity within a system, and a CPM graphically represents one process.

Operation

An *operation* corresponds most closely to the meaning of process in other methods. Within an area of activity, there is a set of operations which lead to one or several results in response to demands of one or more events external to the system (Quang and Chartier-Kastler 1991).

An operation is graphically represented by a rectangle within which its name is shown. Figure 10.6 shows an example of an operation. An operation is triggered by the occurrence of an event. By definition, once an operation is triggered it cannot stop or attend to other events until all its tasks are terminated (Tardieu *et al.* 1983).

Task

A *task* represents a unitary action executed within a system (Quang and Chartier-Kastler 1991), and it is a detailed action of an operation.

Tasks do not have to be shown on the CPM. In some cases, however, when the number of tasks defined is small, their names are written under the name of the operation inside the operation box (Collongues *et al.* 1989). If they are not shown on the CPM they must be written on a document as an appendix to the CPM. Examples of task names can be seen in Figure 10.6.

EVENT

IE

For IE, an *event* is the trigger for a process, and it is defined as: 'a significant occurrence, initiated by external agents or by the passage of time which triggers a process, that must be recognised and responded to' (Martin 1990).

Figure 10.7 Event payment triggering the Check payment process (IE).

External event   Internal event

Figure 10.8 A job request from a customer is an external event, and a customer balance produced by a system is an internal event (MERISE).

All events are external to a process and their duration is not defined. An event, which appears in the process dependency and data flow diagrams, is represented by a large arrow pointing towards the process that it triggers, as shown in Figure 10.7.

MERISE

For MERISE, two types of event exist. One is termed an *external event* because it is produced in the environment and represents the initiation of a process. The second is termed an *internal event* because it takes place when an operation is finished (Rochfeld and Tardieu 1983). An internal event is also termed 'result' (Collongues *et al.* 1989), and it may trigger another operation or process.

An event is the carrier of properties, and its duration is infinite, unless it is the last event to comply with the condition which triggers an operation, in which case the duration of the event is zero.

An event in MERISE is represented graphically by an oval figure within which its name is written. To distinguish between the two types of events, a shadow pattern is used to represent an external event, while the absence of such a pattern represents an internal event, as seen in Figure 10.8.

DATA FLOW

IE

In IE, a data flow is termed a *link* as it joins two processes. However, the data associated with the link is not specified. A link appears in the process dependency and process data flow diagrams and is graphically represented by a line which joins

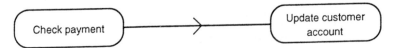

Figure 10.9 Data flow between Check payment process and Update customer account process (IE).

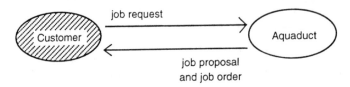

Figure 10.10 A customer makes a job request to Aquaduct, and Aquaduct sends a job proposal and job order to the customer (MERISE).

the two related processes. In the middle of the line a small arrow is drawn indicating the direction of the flow. An example is shown in Figure 10.9.

MERISE

Flow diagram

In MERISE, the exchange of information among different actors is represented by a *flow*. A flow appears only on the flow diagram and it is represented graphically by a line with an arrowhead to show the direction of the flow. The flow description, which may refer to the medium carrying the information, is given next to the line that represents the flow. Figure 10.10 shows an example.

Conceptual processing model

The term *data flow* is also used in the CPM, and data flow is represented by a plain line which joins an operation to the event(s) which initiates it or which results from it. The content of a data flow is not described on the CPM, but it contains information related to the event and, if it joins an initiating event to an operation, is identified with a lower-case letter. An example of two such data flows, a and b, can be seen in Figure 10.11.

The figure shows that, when the reminder and amount external events occur, they supply two data flows and initiate the operation Check supplier account. This may generate two events, debt and inconsistent reminder, with accompanying data flows.

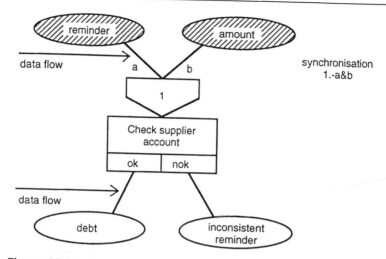

Figure 10.11   Data flows, an operation and events in a CPM (MERISE).

The a and b identifiers are combined (as a & b) to describe the conditions for event synchronisation (see below), and ok and nok are used to evaluate the result of the operation and are known as issuing rules (see below).

As may be seen for the debt and inconsistent reminder events, it is not the convention in MERISE to identify the data flows which are generated from an operation and which accompany events. However, the data flows may be identified if such events provide data to later operations. This will be seen in the case study solution in the next chapter.

DATA STORE

IE

A *data store* is represented in the process data flow diagram only and it represents the source or destination of information for a process. A data store is represented graphically by an open-ended rectangle with its name written inside. Figure 10.12 shows an example.

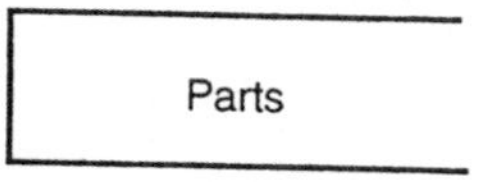

Parts

Figure 10.12   Data store parts (IE).

MERISE

MERISE does not represent data stores.

CONTROL STRUCTURES

Definitions

Control structures consist of different types of relations which exist between processes. The basic control structures and their meanings are:

- *Sequence.* Whether a given process should execute and finish before another process starts.

- *Selection.* One of a set of processes should be executed only if a given condition applies.

- *Iteration.* A process is repeated until the condition for termination of the repetition is met.

- *Concurrency.* A process may be executed at the same time as another process.

IE

In IE there are four types of rule which correspond to control structures, that may be represented in the different diagrams: dependency, cardinality constraint, mutual exclusivity and concurrency.

Dependency

This rule is concerned with modelling *sequence*, as dependency represents the sequence in which a set of processes must be executed. For example, process B is dependent on process A where process B cannot be executed until process A has terminated.

Three different types of dependency among different processes are provided:

1. *One process dependent on one other process.* This is the situation where several processes exist, but the second process cannot be performed until the first process has terminated, and the third process cannot be performed until the

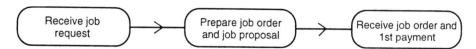

Figure 10.13 The Prepare job order and job proposal process cannot be performed until a job request has been received. To receive a job order and 1st payment, a job order and job proposal must have been prepared (IE).

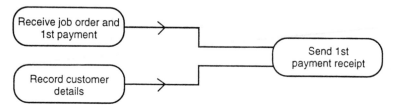

Figure 10.14 Send 1st payment receipt is performed when Receive job order and 1st payment and Record customer details processes have terminated (IE).

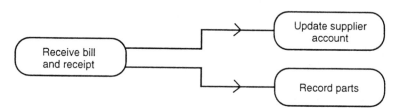

Figure 10.15 Update supplier account and Record parts processes are executed when Receive bill and receipt has terminated (IE).

second process has terminated and so on. An example can be seen in Figure 10.13.

2. *One process dependent on many processes.* This is where several independent processes are linked to the dependent process, as in Figure 10.14.

3. *Many processes dependent on one process.* This is where one process is linked to several dependent processes, as in Figure 10.15.

Cardinality

The cardinality rule is concerned with the *selection* and *iteration* control structures.

It is used to specify how many times a process A may be executed in the context of its dependency relationship R(AB) with another process B. Process A may

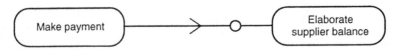

Figure 10.16 Elaborate supplier balance process (optional) may or may not be executed after the Make payment process (IE).

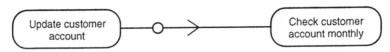

Figure 10.17 Update customer account process (optional) may or may not be executed before the Check customer account monthly process (IE).

either precede or follow the execution of process B. The cardinality style in IE is the lookacross style (Ferg 1991).

The cardinality of a process is specified in terms of *minimum* and *maximum cardinality* indicators. The values that the minimum cardinality indicator can take are 0 or 1, and the values that the maximum cardinality indicator can take are 1 or N, where N means many (one or more than one).

Minimum cardinality indicator

This is concerned with the *selection* control structure. The minimum cardinality of process A represents whether or not process B must execute in the context of R(AB). When the minimum cardinality indicator = 0, process B is termed 'optional', and process B may or may not be performed either before or after the execution of process A.

If the minimum cardinality indicator = 1, process B is termed 'mandatory', and process B must be executed either before or after the execution of process A.

The optional execution of process B in the context of R(AB) is represented by a small circle nearest process B placed across the line representing R(AB). Figure 10.16 shows an example of the optional execution of a dependent process, and Figure 10.17 shows the optional execution of a preceding process.

The mandatory execution of process B in the context of R(AB) is represented by a short line nearest process B placed at right angles across the line representing R(AB). Figure 10.18 shows an example of the mandatory execution of a dependent process, and Figure 10.19 shows the mandatory execution of a preceding process.

Maximum cardinality indicator

This is concerned with the *iteration* control structure. For process A, when the maximum cardinality indicator = 1, process B may be executed within the context of R(AB) at most once either before or after the execution of process A. If the

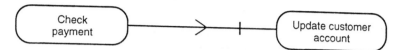

Figure 10.18 Update customer account process (mandatory) must be executed after the Check payment process (IE).

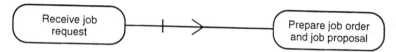

Figure 10.19 Receive job request process (mandatory) must be executed before the Prepare job order and job proposal process (IE).

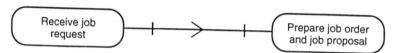

Figure 10.20 For the Receive job request process, there is only one associated Prepare job order and job proposal process and for the Prepare job order and job proposal process there is only one associated Receive job request process (IE).

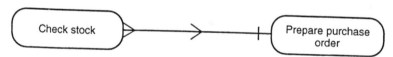

Figure 10.21 The Check stock process may be followed by only one Prepare purchase order process, and the Prepare purchase order may be preceded by many Check stock processes (IE).

maximum cardinality indicator = N, process B may be executed once or more than once either before or after the execution of process A.

To graphically represent a process A with maximum cardinality indicator = 1, a short line nearest process B is placed at right angles across the line representing R(AB). This is shown in Figure 10.20. A 'crow's foot' is used similarly, in Figure 10.21, to represent the fact that process A has a maximum cardinality indicator = N.

In Figure 10.21, the Prepare purchase order process has a maximum cardinality of N, while the Check stock process has a maximum cardinality of 1, in the context of this dependency relationship.

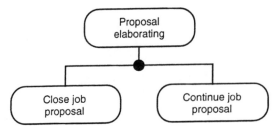

Figure 10.22 *Mutual exclusivity rule in a process decomposition diagram. For the Proposal elaborating decomposed process, only one of the two resulting processes may be executed (IE).*

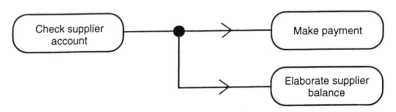

Figure 10.23 *Mutual exclusivity rule in a process dependency diagram. After the Check supplier account process, either Make payment or Elaborate supplier balance can be executed but not both (IE).*

Mutual exclusivity

This is concerned with the *selection* control structure. Sometimes, only one of several processes may be performed. To show the alternatives, the mutual exclusivity rule is used.

In a decomposition diagram, the mutual exclusivity rule is represented by a dot placed on the line which joins a parent process with its child processes, as shown in Figure 10.22.

In dependency and data flow diagrams, the dot is placed on the line which joins one process with several alternate dependent processes (Figure 10.23), or several alternate processes with one dependent process (Figure 10.24).

Concurrency

Concurrency refers to the situation where processes may be performed at the same time. In decomposition diagrams, concurrency is represented by an arc placed on the line which joins child processes to the parent process. In dependency and data flow diagrams, the arc is placed on the line which joins dependent processes to the preceding process. This is shown in Figure 10.25.

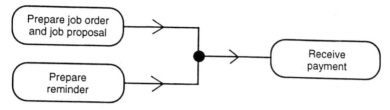

Figure 10.24 The Receive payment process may occur after either the Prepare job order and job proposal process, or the Prepare reminder process, but not both (IE).

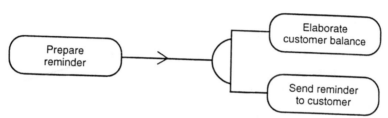

Figure 10.25 The Elaborate customer balance and Send reminder to customer processes may be executed at the same time, following the execution of the Prepare reminder process (IE).

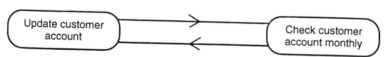

Figure 10.26 Parallel links. When the Update customer account process occurs the Check customer account monthly process may also occur, checking the same account (IE).

Parallel links

A fifth type of rule in IE is *parallel links*, which refers to a feedback mechanism between two processes. This is represented by two links between the same two processes with the arrows in the middle of the links set in opposite directions, as in Figure 10.26. No control structure is modelled by this rule.

MERISE

In the CPM, three concepts are used to model control structure: synchronisation rule, issuing rule and data flow.

Synchronisation rule

This rule is concerned with the *selection* control structure. A synchronisation is defined as a condition which must be satisfied in order to initiate an operation (Tardieu *et al.* 1983), and it is specified in terms of the data flow(s) that accompany an event or events.

A synchronisation is composed of the operators 'and', 'or' and negation. The life cycle of a synchronisation is determined by the occurrence of the first event and the occurrence of the last event defined in the condition. When several events are described in the condition, the occurrence of the first event sets the synchronisation to a waiting state until the occurrence of the last event which closes the synchronisation life cycle. The occurrences of the events are not restricted to any sequence.

The synchronisation of an operation is graphically represented by a five-sided symbol containing a condition identifier (usually a number), with the condition specification described, using the identifier, at the top of the diagram.

Figure 10.27 shows an example where the Check supplier account operation is initiated by the occurrence of the reminder and amount events.

The a and b data flow identifiers (a identifies the data flow containing information about the reminder, and b identifies the data flow containing information about the amount) are used to describe the condition in the synchronisation which must be true for the operation to be initiated. In this example, they are combined (as a & b) to describe the conditions for event synchronisation.

Issuing rule

This rule is also concerned with the *selection* control structure. Issuing rules are those rules which are applied to the results of an operation (Collongues *et al.* 1989). The set of all the issuing rules of an operation must cover the set of all possible cases, such that the operation always produces a result.

An issuing rule is often simplified diagrammatically to the ok and nok predicates. The ok predicate is true if the result of an operation is satisfactory, while the nok predicate is true if the result of an operation is unsatisfactory. Depending on the outcome of the application of the rules, an event or events will be generated with accompanying data flow(s).

The issuing rule predicates are graphically represented below the operation box, with details specified in a document attached to the diagram. Figure 10.27 shows an example of issuing rules applied to the result of the Check supplier account operation.

Once the operation has terminated, the results are validated. The detailed tasks of this operation may specify, for the ok rule, that if the reminder and the amount both agree with the amount owed to the supplier then the internal event debt is produced. The nok rule may specify that, if the amount owed is inconsistent with the reminder, then the internal event inconsistent reminder is produced.

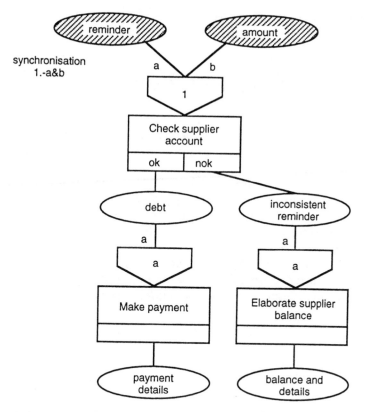

Figure 10.27 *Synchronisation and issuing rules in MERISE.*

Synchronisation and issuing rules are based on the concepts of pre- and postconditions, where preconditions set the rules for an operation to begin execution, and postconditions govern the states that may result at termination of the operation.

Data flow

Data flow and its direction is used to model *iteration* and *sequence*. A data flow, represented by a line, which accompanies an event generated by an operation, may be input to any CPM operation, and hence is used to model iteration and sequence. An example of the modelling of sequence is shown in Figure 10.27.

If the inconsistent reminder event is generated by the Check supplier account process, the Elaborate supplier balance operation will be next in sequence to be initiated. Alternatively, if the debt event is generated, then the next operation to be initiated will be Make payment.

An example of iteration in the MERISE case study solution is shown in Figure 12.6 in Chapter 12.

ENTITY LIFE HISTORY (ELH) IN SSADM

In this section, we present the entity life history (ELH) as the part of the process model in SSADM that shows control structures. An ELH shows the life cycle of an entity by describing the events and related conditions that affect a particular instance of the entity.

For each entity in the entity model an ELH is constructed, and the events specified are those which trigger update processes only. Graphically, an ELH is represented by a hierarchy of rectangular boxes in which the box at the top of the diagram represents the entity instance, and the leaves represent the different events which affect the instance. An example is shown in Figure 10.28.

An ELH also defines rules to control the effect of events on an entity instance, the first four of which correspond to the concept of control structure. The rules are: sequence, selection, iteration, parallel structures and quit and resume.

Sequence

This relates to the sequence in which events must occur, commonly viewed as representing the birth, main life and death of an entity instance. Birth represents the creation of an entity instance in the system. Life represents the events which trigger the processes to update information about the entity instance, and death represents the end of interest of the system in the entity instance.

This means that where there is a *total* time ordering of a set of events on a particular entity instance, the ELH can model this precisely. By total time ordering we mean that each event occurs either before or after another event, and no event occurs at the same time as another event.

Sequence is graphically represented by events shown in a left to right sequence, as shown in Figure 10.28. The job order and 1st payment event initiates the creation of an instance of the customer entity in the system. The transactions event represents the main life of the entity, and the end of job event represents the death of the instance.

Selection

When more than one event affects an entity, it is possible that either one of the events may happen, but not both. This is graphically represented by a small circle placed at the right-hand side top of the box representing the event. Figure 10.28 shows that either the debt condition or the no debt condition may happen, but not both.

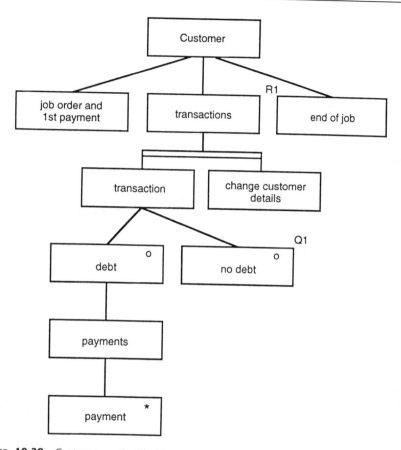

Figure 10.28 *Customer entity life history showing sequence, iteration, selection, parallel structures, and quit and resume (SSADM).*

Iteration

This rule expresses the fact that an event may occur more than once. Each iteration must be terminated before the next one starts. This is represented by an asterisk placed at the right-hand side top of the box representing the event. Figure 10.28 shows that the payment event may happen more than once.

Parallel structures

This rule defines the events whose sequence cannot be predicted. That is, in many cases, there is only a *partial* time ordering of a set of events and this cannot be modelled precisely. By partial time ordering we mean that some event may occur at the same time as another event.

Figure 10.28 shows that the change customer details event may happen at any time relative to a transaction event.

Quit and resume

This type of structure indicates the escape from a normal pattern of events when an exception occurs. Many quits may be associated with one resume.

The letter 'Q' is used to represent a quit and it is placed at the right-hand side on top of the box representing the event that causes the quit, and a number is given to identify it. Resume is represented by a letter 'R', placed at the left-hand side on top of the box representing the event that resumes from the quit, and it carries the same number identifier as the associated quit. Figure 10.28 shows an example where, after a no debt event happens, the following event that occurs is the end of job event.

To summarise the customer ELH in Figure 10.28, the first event is job order and 1st payment, and then either the debt or no debt condition may occur, but not both. If the debt event occurs, then the payment event is next, which may happen more than once. During this time, the change customer details event may also occur. The end of job event is the next to occur. When the no debt event occurs, the next event is the end of job event.

SUMMARY

We have presented the concepts of the IE and MERISE process models illustrated by examples from the case study, and we also described the SSADM Entity Life History.

Concepts

Tables 10.1 and 10.2 summarise the process modelling concepts provided by the methods, considering the ELH only for SSADM. The methods have partial correspondences only for process and control structure. No method provides the concepts of external entity. IE and SSADM provide a control structure for concurrency while MERISE does not.

Viewpoints

Overview

Table 10.1 is an unsatisfactory basis for comparison as, in process modelling, methods aim to provide different *viewpoints* by selecting certain concepts and showing these on different types of diagrams.

Table 10.1 *Process modelling concepts in IE, MERISE and SSADM ELH*

Concept	Method					
	IE	**Term**	**MERISE**	**Term**	**SSADM ELH**	**Term**
External entity	–		–	actor only in flow diagram	–	
Process	yes	process	yes	process, operation & task	(yes)	event
Event	yes	event	yes	internal & external event	–	
Data flow	yes	link (unlabelled)	yes	data flow (unlabelled)	–	
Data store	yes	data store	–		–	
Control structure	yes	see Table 10.2	(yes)	see Table 10.2	yes	see Table 10.7

Table 10.2 *Control structures in IE, MERISE and SSADM*

Control structures	**IE**	**MERISE**	**SSADM**
Sequence	Dependency (in process dependency diagram)	Data flow	Sequence
Selection	Minimum cardinality Mutual exclusivity (in process decomposition diagram, dependency diagram and data flow diagram)	Synchronisation and issuing rules	Selection
Iteration	Maximum cardinality (in dependency diagram and data flow diagram)	Data flow	Iteration
Concurrency	Concurrency (in dependency diagram and data flow diagram)	–	Parallel structures

We define viewpoint as follows:

> A viewpoint is a perspective over a system consisting of specific concepts and relationships between these concepts

Different viewpoints are important as there are, for example, different perspectives which are suited for managers as opposed to employees of an organisation.

Definition of viewpoints

We define the following viewpoints:

1. *Decomposition*. This viewpoint shows processes decomposed to their lowest level of detail. It consists of processes and the 'part-of' relationships between those processes.

2. *Data flow*. The flow of data is shown consisting of processes (level 1), processes and data stores (level 2) and processes, data stores and external entities (level 3).

3. *Behavioural*. Processes and control structure are shown.

4. *State transition*. Object states and related transitions are shown in terms of objects and update processes (level 1), and objects, update processes and control structure (level 2).

It is more informative to compare methods by the viewpoints they provide. Table 10.3 shows the viewpoints and their associated diagrams provided by IE, MERISE and SSADM (ELH only). We do not consider the flow diagram of MERISE as it contains very little information.

Table 10.3 Viewpoints provided by IE, MERISE and SSADM ELH

| | Method | | |
Viewpoint	IE	MERISE	SSADM
Decomposition	process decomposition diagram	–	–
Behavioural	process dependency diagram	CPM	(ELH)
Data flow	process data flow diagram (level 2)	CPM (level 1)	–
State transition	–	–	ELH (level 2)

Viewpoint comparison

Decomposition
IE shows processes to any level of detail but MERISE only allows two levels of process (CPM and operation). Below this level, MERISE would have to use diagrams on the logical design level.

Behavioural
Both IE and MERISE provide this viewpoint. It is partial for SSADM as the ELH specifies only update processes.

Data flow

This viewpoint is only partially provided in MERISE (level 1) as data stores and external entities are not modelled. This means that MERISE does not show, in contrast to an IE process DFD, whether a process receives data directly from a preceding process, or whether there is a time delay indicated by the fact that data is received from a data store.

IE (level 2) omits external entities from its data flow viewpoint.

State transition

The ELH of SSADM provides this for each entity type at level 2 as control structures are also specified.

Graphical representations

A surface difference between IE and MERISE is the graphical representation of the concepts. Table 10.4 shows the graphical representation of the concepts that IE and MERISE define, the representation of control structures in IE is shown in Table 10.5, Figure 10.29 shows the control structures of MERISE and Table 10.6 shows the graphical representation of the SSADM rules, including control structure.

Table 10.4 Graphical representation of concepts in IE and MERISE methods

Concept	IE	MERISE
External entity	does not exist	does not exist
Process	Close job proposal	Close job proposal
Event	payment	payment (external event) balance (internal event)
Data flow	A → B	→ in flow diagram — in CPM
Data store	Parts	does not exist

Table 10.5 Graphical representation of control structures in IE

Control structure	Representation

Dependency

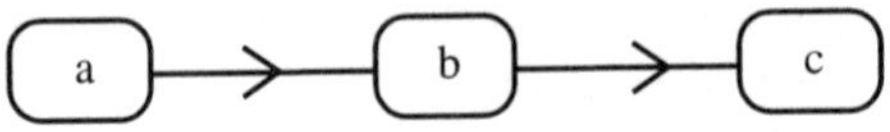

string of dependent processes

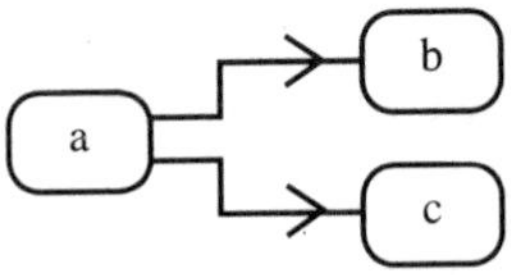

many processes dependent on one process

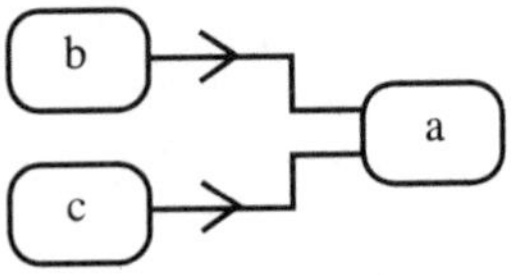

one process dependent on many processes

Cardinality

a optional   b mandatory

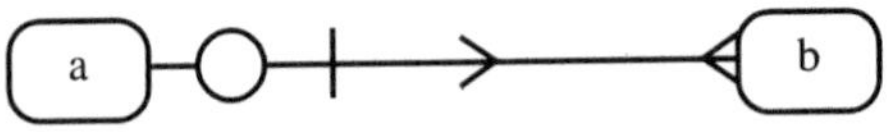

A   maximum cardinality=N
B   maximum cardinality=1

Mutual exclusivity

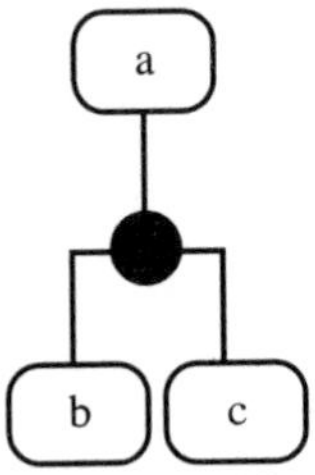

in decomposition diagram

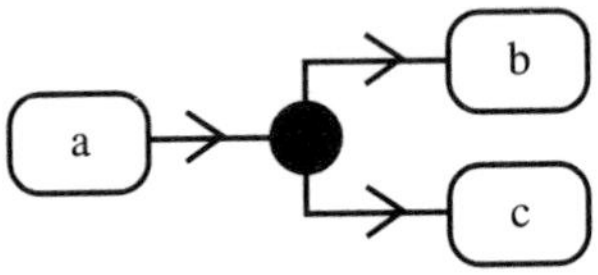

in dependency diagram and data flow diagram

Concurrency

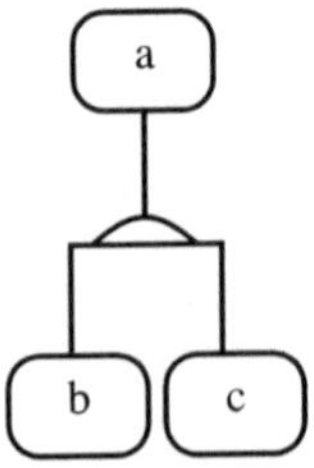

in decomposition diagram

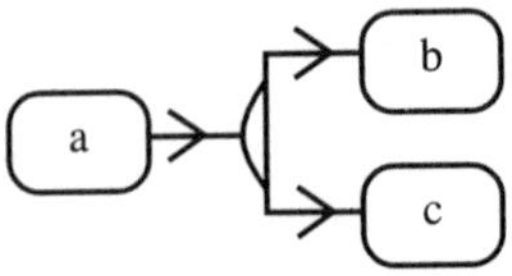

in dependency diagram and data flow diagram

Table 10.6 Rules in SSADM and graphical representation

Rule	Graphical representation

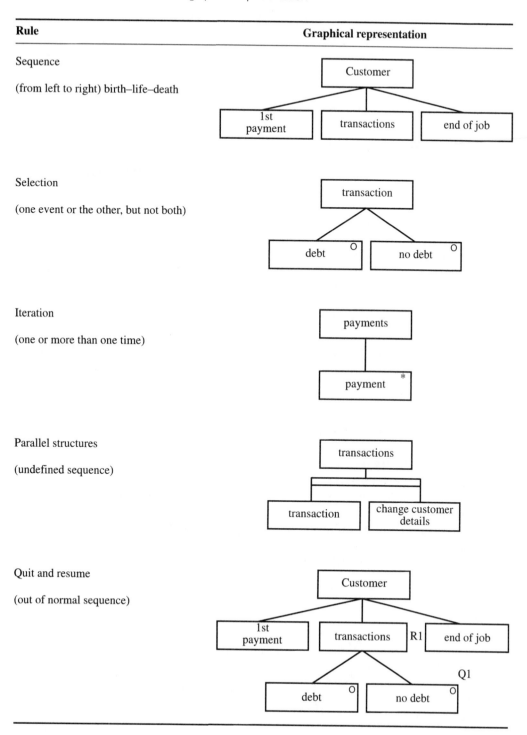

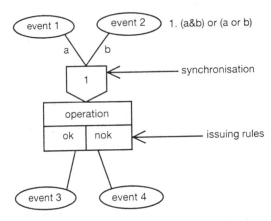

Figure 10.29 Graphical representation of control structures in MERISE

CONCLUSIONS

Reference framework concepts

Tables 10.1 and 10.2 show that no method provides all the concepts, and no method corresponds to any other with respect to the concepts that it provides. No method provides the external entity concept.

Reference framework viewpoints

Table 10.3 shows that no method provides exactly similar viewpoints.

For process modelling, the methods display wide differences, both in the concepts and diagrams that they provide and the viewpoints which the diagrams are intended to express. In addition, different approaches to process modelling have been revealed. For example, MERISE is an event-based approach to process modelling, which is significantly different to IE, and this approach may be preferred by some developers.

Chapter 11

CASE STUDY – DISCUSSION AND PROCESS MODEL SOLUTION IN IE

This chapter consists of two sections:

I. In the first section, comments are made on a range of topics which assist the understanding of the case study process model solution in IE.

II. In the second section, the process model solution in IE is presented. This consists of (a) process decomposition diagrams, (b) process dependency diagrams, (c) process data flow diagrams.

   The data dictionary and case study text with requirements tracing from Chapter 9 also form part of the solution.

I. COMMENTS ON CASE STUDY SOLUTION

This section discusses several topics which cover general issues in building IE process models, as well as making comments on various aspects of the specific models presented in Section II.

GENERAL POINTS

As for DFD-based modelling in Chapter 9, the aim of the process model is user-centred.

Previous solutions

As for the DFD solution, a structure model is required to be integrated into the process model and this is done with the data dictionary described in Chapter 9. The data dictionary is common to all the methods and is an implicit part of the IE case study solution. Similarly, the case study text in Chapter 9, containing process names by text paragraphs, may also be used to help understand the process model.

HOW TO BUILD AN IE PROCESS MODEL

How to build a process decomposition diagram

You should follow the same guidelines as those established in Chapter 9 for identifying processes. The next step is to draw the diagram on its hierarchical levels, decomposing each process until the elementary processes have been reached. The final step is to add any mutual exclusivity or minimum cardinality rules that may apply.

How to build a process dependency diagram

A high-level process from the process decomposition diagram should be selected and then the IE rules discussed in Chapter 10 should be applied to its constituent processes in the following order:

1. Arrange processes in the horizontal plane based on their dependencies, so that they are read from left to right.

2. Arrange processes in the vertical plane based on their mutual exclusivity.

3. Place concurrent and parallel processes near to one another.

4. Add minimum and maximum cardinality to the processes.

The last step is to add events to the processes which they initiate.

How to build a process data flow diagram

Once a process dependency diagram is available the process data flow diagram is built by adding data stores and data flows.

Control structure implied in case study text

To reduce the amount of detail in the case study text, we have not been explicit about the minimum and maximum cardinalities between pairs of processes. To provide examples of IE modelling in this respect, a few examples have been inferred from the text.

II. CASE STUDY SOLUTION – PROCESS MODEL IN IE

This section presents the IE process model solution for the case study, consisting of the process decomposition, dependency and data flow diagrams. We also provide a commentary on the diagrams.

In addition, the case study text in Chapter 9 contains requirements tracing between the text and the process model, and the data dictionary showing data stores and their contents in Chapter 9 should also be consulted.

High-level process decomposition diagram

Figure 11.1 shows the three main application areas of the case study in a process decomposition diagram, showing them as processes that are decomposed further.

Proposal elaborating process

Process decomposition diagram

Figure 11.2 shows the exploded Proposal elaborating process with elementary processes.

The Close job proposal and Continue job proposal processes are linked by the mutual exclusivity rule, which indicates that one process, but not both, may be executed.

Process dependency diagram

Figure 11.3 shows that the Send proposal and 1st payment receipt process is dependent on two independent processes, Receive job order and 1st payment and Record customer details.

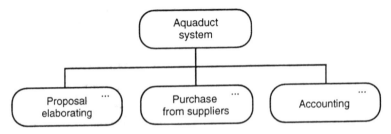

Figure 11.1 Process decomposition diagram of Aquaduct showing processes which are decomposed further (IE).

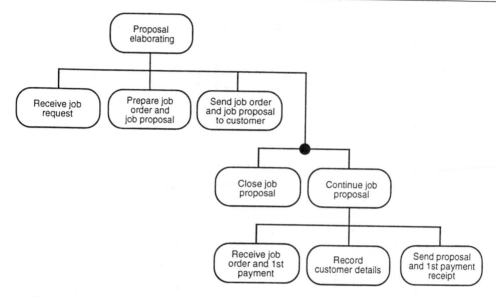

Figure 11.2   Process decomposition diagram showing exploded Proposal elaborating process with elementary processes (IE).

The figure also shows that this group of processes, and the Close job proposal process, are linked by the mutual exclusivity rule, which indicates that either but not both may be executed.

Another feature is the maximum cardinality of 1 for the Receive job request and Prepare job order and job proposal processes. There is also a minimum cardinality of 1 for the Prepare job order and job proposal process. Thus, the Prepare job order and job proposal process must be preceded by one execution only of the Receive job request process. Several events are shown by the processes they trigger.

Process data flow diagram

Figure 11.4 shows the mutual exclusivity rule for the Close job proposal process and the dependent processes beginning with the Receive job order and 1st payment process.

The events job request, parts defined, rejection and 1st payment and job order are shown next to the processes they trigger.

Purchase from supplier process

Process decomposition diagram

Figure 11.5 shows the decomposition of this process, and also shows that Record parts and Purchase stock are mutually exclusive processes.

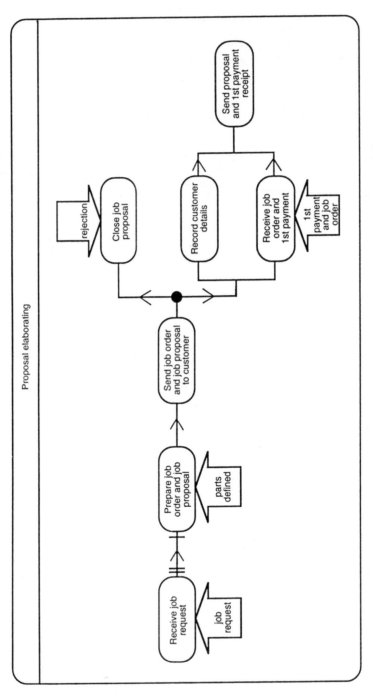

Figure 11.3 Process dependency diagram for the Proposal elaborating process (IE).

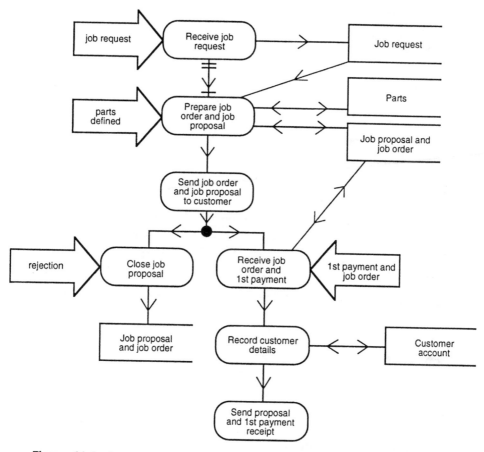

Figure 11.4 Process data flow diagram for the Proposal elaborating process (IE).

Process dependency diagram

Figure 11.6 shows a maximum cardinality of many for the Send purchase order to supplier and Receive bill and receipt processes. Also shown is a maximum cardinality of many for the Prepare purchase order process and a maximum cardinality of 1 for the Check stock process.

The Prepare purchase order process may thus be preceded by many executions of the Check stock process.

The figure also shows mutually exclusive process dependencies after the Check stock process.

Process data flow diagram

Figure 11.7 shows two mutually exclusive process dependencies involving the processes Prepare purchase order and Record parts. A maximum cardinality of

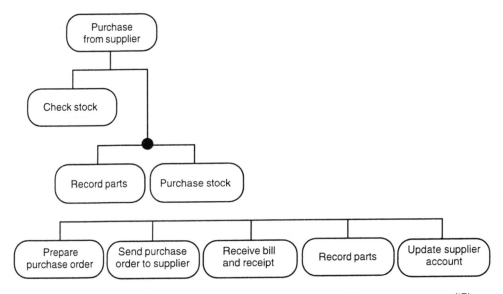

Figure 11.5 *Exploded Purchase from supplier process with elementary processes (IE).*

many is also shown for the Send purchase order to supplier and Receive bill and receipt processes.

Accounting process

Process decomposition diagram

Figure 11.8 shows two groups of mutually exclusive processes concerning Make payment and Check balance, and Monthly action and End of job action.

Process dependency diagram

Figure 11.9 shows concurrency between Elaborate customer balance and Send reminder to customer.

The diagram also shows a minimum cardinality of zero for two processes, Make payment and Prepare reminder, and a maximum cardinality of many for Elaborate supplier balance, Make payment and Prepare reminder processes.

Thus, the Elaborate supplier balance process does not necessarily have to be executed after the Make payment process has executed.

Parallel links exist between Check customer account monthly and Update customer account processes. The process Send balance and details to accountant is a process dependent on two processes.

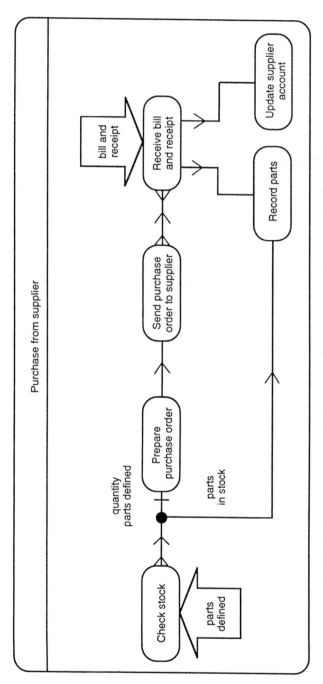

Figure 11.6   Process dependency diagram for the Purchase from supplier process (IE).

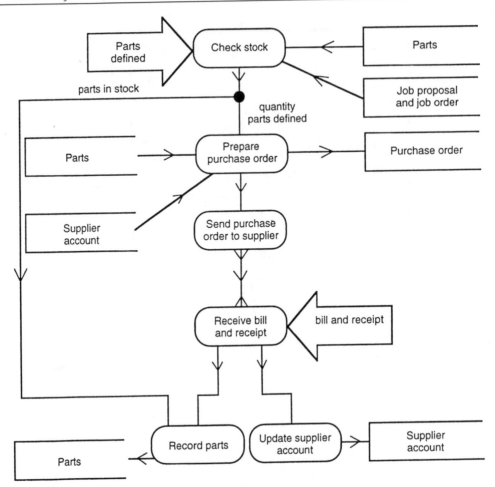

Figure 11.7 Process data flow diagram for the Purchase from supplier process (IE).

Process data flow diagram

Figure 11.10 shows concurrency between the Elaborate customer balance and Send reminder to customer processes.

The diagram also shows a minimum cardinality of zero of three processes, Prepare reminder, Make payment and Check customer account monthly. A minimum cardinality of 1 exists for the Check payment process, meaning that the Update customer account process must be executed after it. There is also a maximum cardinality of many for the Elaborate supplier balance, Make payment and Prepare reminder processes, in other process dependency relationships.

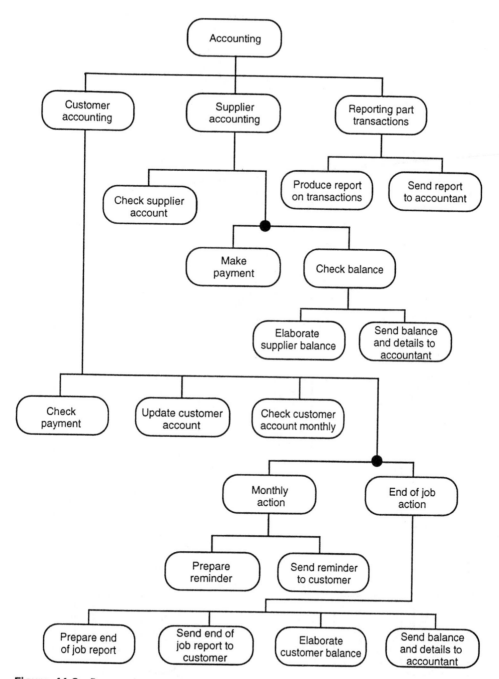

Figure 11.8 Process decomposition diagram for the Accounting process showing different levels of decomposition and elementary processes (IE).

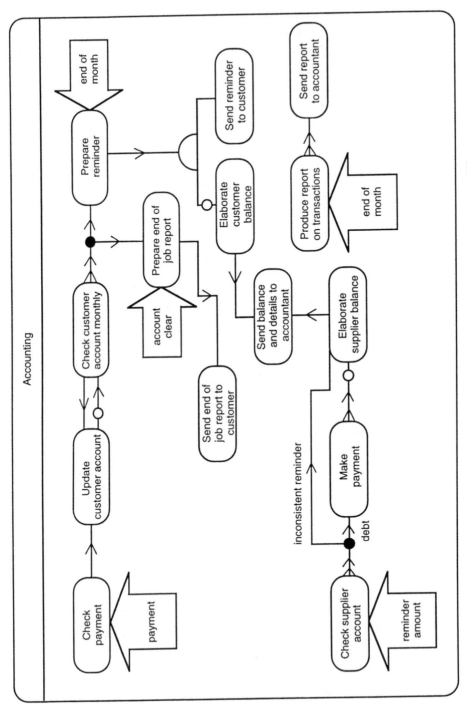

Figure 11.9 Process dependency diagram for the Accounting process (IE).

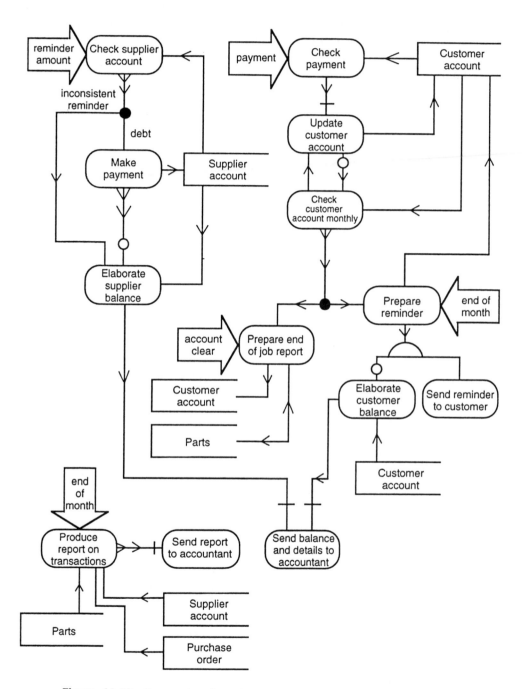

Figure 11.10   Process data flow diagram for the Accounting process (IE).

Parallel links exist between Check customer account monthly and Update customer account processes, and the process Send balance and details to accountant is dependent on two processes, Elaborate customer balance, and Elaborate supplier balance.

Mandatory processes are Send report to accountant, Send balance and details to accountant and Update customer account.

Chapter 12

CASE STUDY – DISCUSSION AND PROCESS MODEL SOLUTION IN MERISE

This chapter consists of two sections:

I.   In the first section, comments are made on a range of topics which assist the understanding of the case study process model solution in MERISE.

II. In the second section, the process model solution in MERISE is presented. This consists of (a) flow diagram and (b) conceptual processing models. In addition, the case study text with requirements tracing is available in Chapter 9.

I. COMMENTS ON CASE STUDY SOLUTION

This section discusses several topics which cover general issues in building MERISE process models, as well as making comments on various aspects of the specific models presented in Section II.

GENERAL POINTS

As for DFD-based modelling, the aim of the process model is user-centred.

Structure model

Although there is a structure model for MERISE it cannot be integrated into the process model as the interaction between process and data is not shown in the process model. No data stores are shown and data flows are indicated only by lower case letters. Thus the data dictionary is not used by MERISE. However, the case study text in Chapter 9, containing process names by text paragraphs, may be used.

HOW TO BUILD A MERISE PROCESS MODEL

How to build a conceptual processing model (CPM)

The first step is to choose the main application or activity areas, as for the other methods. Each is represented by a process and a CPM is assigned to each.

For the MERISE case study solution we have chosen areas that match the high-level processes of other method solutions. The areas are: proposal elaborating, purchase from supplier, customer accounting, supplier accounting and parts accounting.

For each CPM, proceed as follows:

1. Identify all the data flows that can occur in this CPM. A rough flow diagram may be used for this.
2. Order the flows starting with the one that triggers the process.
3. Make each flow into an event.
4. Decide on the operations that make up the CPM.
5. Decide, for each operation, synchronisation and issuing rules. Draw and label the data flows connecting events to issuing and synchronisation rules.

II. CASE STUDY SOLUTION – PROCESS MODEL IN MERISE

This section presents the MERISE process model solution for the case study, consisting of the flow diagram and conceptual processing models. We also provide a commentary on the diagrams.

MERISE PROCESS MODEL

Flow diagram

Figure 12.1 shows the external entities and their main flows to and from the Aquaduct system.

Proposal elaborating CPM

Figure 12.2 shows that the occurrence of the external event job request is accompanied by a data flow a. The synchronisation rule in the five-sided figure for the Receive job request operation shows that the presence of this data flow is required to initiate this operation.

If the nok issuing rule governing the result of this operation is true then the internal event rejection is generated.

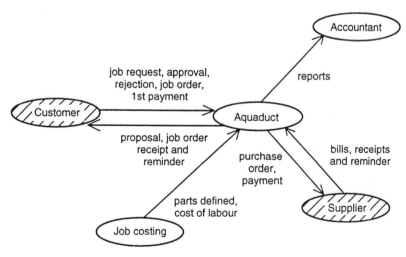

Figure 12.1 Aquaduct system flow diagram (MERISE).

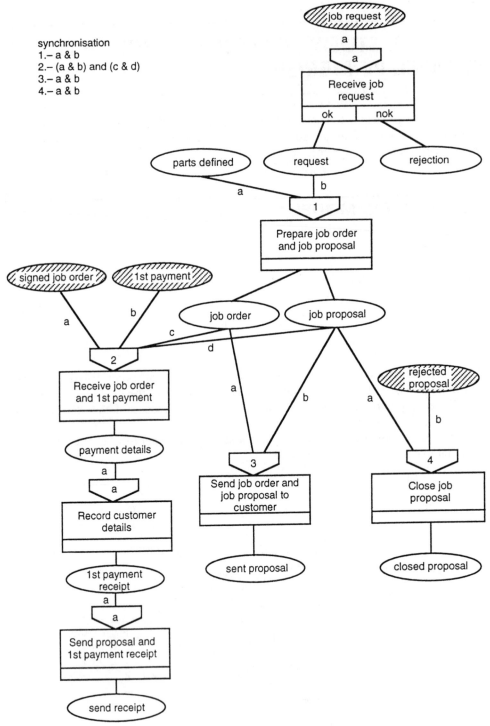

synchronisation
1.– a & b
2.– (a & b) and (c & d)
3.– a & b
4.– a & b

Figure 12.2 Proposal elaborating Conceptual Processing Model (MERISE).

If the ok issuing rule is true the event request is generated, which is accompanied by a data flow b. When the parts defined event occurs, accompanied by a data flow a, the synchronisation rule ('1') for the Prepare job order and job proposal operation shows that both a and b data flows should occur to initiate this operation.

If the result is ok the events job order and job proposal are generated.

The Close job proposal operation is initiated if the job proposal and rejected proposal events occur, as the relevant synchronisation rule ('4') is that a and b data flows should occur. These data flows accompany these two events. The closed proposal event is generated.

The Send job order and job proposal to customer operation is initiated if the job proposal and job order events occur, as the relevant synchronisation rule ('3') is that a and b data flows should occur. The sent proposal event is generated.

The Receive job order and 1st payment operation is initiated if the job proposal, job order, signed job order and 1st payment events occur, as the relevant synchronisation rule ('2') requires the data flows that accompany all four events to occur.

Subsequent operations have simple synchronisation rules for their initiation, involving one data flow that accompanies the internal event generated from a previous operation.

Purchase from supplier CPM

A summary of the contents of the Purchase from supplier CPM in Figure 12.3 is as follows:

- operations – Check stock, Prepare purchase order, Send purchase order to supplier, Receive bill and receipt, Update supplier account and Record parts;

- external events – receipt and bill;

- internal events – parts defined, no-parts, parts, purchase order, sent order, bill, receipt, debt and new parts;

- synchronisations – a, 1 = (a & b & c), 2 = (a & b), 3 = ((a & b) or c)) or (a & b &c);

- issuing rules – ok and nok;

- data flows – edges with a, b or c, also edges without identifiers.

Customer accounting CPM

Figure 12.4 shows that the occurrence of the external event payment (from a customer) is accompanied by a data flow a, which initiates the Check payment

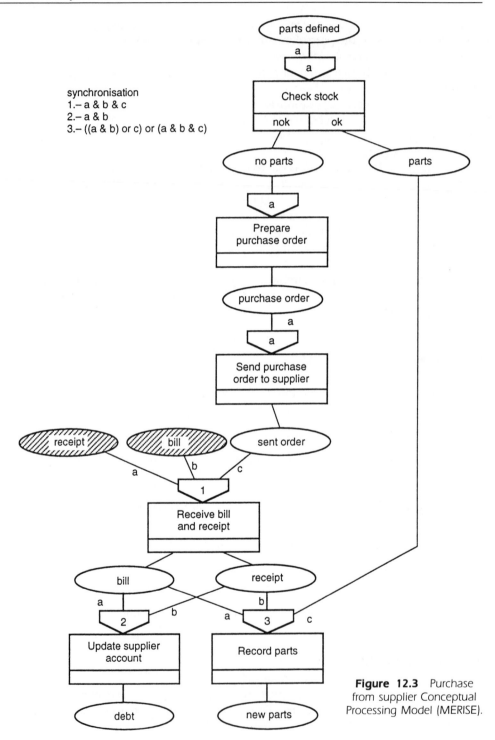

synchronisation
1.– a & b & c
2.– a & b
3.– ((a & b) or c) or (a & b & c)

Figure 12.3 Purchase from supplier Conceptual Processing Model (MERISE).

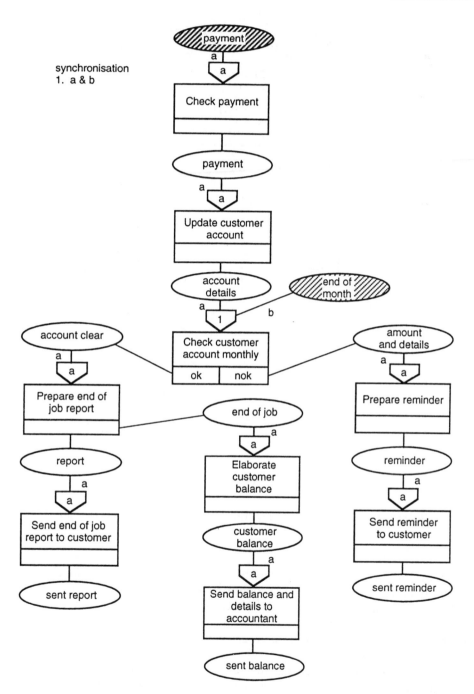

Figure 12.4   *Customer accounting Conceptual Processing Model (MERISE).*

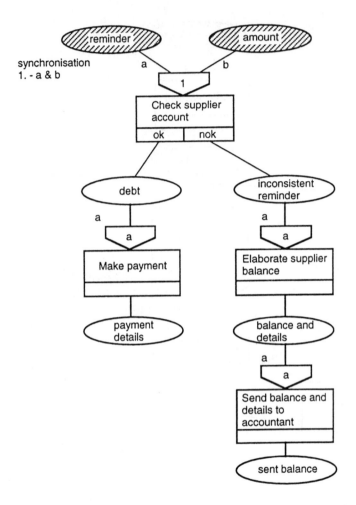

Figure 12.5 *Supplier accounting Conceptual Processing Model (MERISE).*

operation. This generates the payment event which initiates the Update customer account operation, generating the account details event.

The synchronisation rule ('1') for the Check customer account monthly operation is a & b, which means that when the events account details and end of month (external) occur together, with their accompanying data flows a and b, this operation is initiated.

If the ok issuing rule governing the result of this operation is true then the (internal) event account clear is generated. The accompanying data flow a is then input to the Prepare end of job report operation, which generates two events:

1. report, which initiates the Send end of job report to customer operation;

2. end of job, which initiates the Elaborate customer balance operation, and subsequently the Send balance and details to accountant operation.

If the nok issuing rule is true the event amount and details is generated, which is accompanied by a data flow a. This initiates the Prepare reminder operation, generating the reminder event, which initiates the Send reminder to customer operation.

Supplier accounting CPM

Figure 12.5 shows that the occurrence of the external events reminder and amount (from a supplier) is accompanied by data flows a and b. When both of these events occur, the Check supplier account operation is initiated.

If the ok issuing rule governing the result of this operation is true then the (internal) event debt is generated. The accompanying data flow a is then input to the Make payment operation, which generates the payment details event.

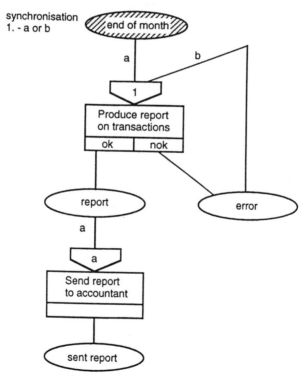

Figure 12.6 Parts accounting Conceptual Processing Model (MERISE).

If the nok issuing rule is true the event inconsistent reminder is generated, which is accompanied by a data flow a. This initiates the Elaborate supplier balance operation, generating the balance and details event, which initiates the Send balance and details to accountant operation.

Parts accounting CPM

Figure 12.6 shows that the occurrence of the external event end of month is accompanied by a data flow a. This initiates the Produce report on transactions and subsequently the Send report to accountant operations. Alternatively, if an error is found after the report has been produced, the nok issuing rule applies and an error event is generated, the associated data flow b causing the report to be produced again.

Chapter 13

METHOD COMPARISON FOR PROCESS MODELLING

In this chapter we compare the reference framework concepts and viewpoints for process modelling with those provided by the methods IE, MERISE, MEIN and SSADM, pointing out correspondences and differences.

CONCEPT COMPARISON

Table 13.1 shows the reference framework concepts provided by the methods for process modelling. An entry in parentheses indicates that provision of a concept is only partial. The table shows that, of the six concepts, only two concepts, process and data flow, have correspondences in all four methods. No method provides the same concepts as any other method. The event concept in the SSADM ELH is regarded as being equivalent to the process reference framework concept.

Table 13.1 Reference framework process modelling concepts in IE, MERISE, MEIN and SSADM

	Method			
Concept	IE	MERISE	MEIN	SSADM
External entity	–	–	yes	yes
Process	yes	yes	yes	yes
Event	yes	yes	–	–
Data flow	yes	yes	yes	yes
Data store	yes	–	yes	yes
Control structure	yes	(yes)	–	(yes)

Table 13.2 *Viewpoints provided by IE, MERISE, MEIN and SSADM*

	Method			
Viewpoint	**IE**	**MERISE**	**MEIN**	**SSADM**
Decomposition	process decomposition diagram	—	(DFD)	(DFD)
Behavioural	process dependency diagram	CPM	—	(ELH)
Data flow	process data flow diagram (level 2)	CPM (level 1)	DFD (level 3)	DFD (level 3)
State transition	—	—	—	ELH (level 2)

VIEWPOINT COMPARISON

Table 13.2 shows the reference framework viewpoints provided by the methods. This allows a more satisfactory basis for determining method correspondences as the viewpoints, expressed in the different diagrams, may be directly compared.

CORRESPONDENCES

MEIN and SSADM

The correspondence between these two methods for the data flow viewpoint, as expressed in the data flow diagram, is one to one for the reference framework concepts. In Chapter 8 we noted that SSADM defines extra detail for data stores and external entities.

DIFFERENCES

All methods

As seen in Table 13.2, no one method provides a similar set of viewpoints to any other method, although the viewpoints of some methods are subsets of the viewpoints provided by others.

SSADM and MEIN do not represent control structures or events in their DFD. They provide a partial decomposition viewpoint only as this must be inferred from the decomposed processes of the DFD. However, they do provide the widest data flow view.

IE and MERISE

Comparing these two methods:

- IE provides the decomposition, behavioural and level 2 data flow viewpoints.

- MERISE allows only the behavioural and level 1 data flow viewpoints, as it does not model data stores or external entities.

- MERISE does not provide the decomposition viewpoint, as it is limited to one level of process decomposition only. This limits the level of abstract detail that it can provide. The Aquaduct case study had only one level of decomposition.

SSADM

The ELH provides the state transition viewpoint, showing update processes on all entity types at level 2, as control structures are provided. No other method provides this. The ELH also provides a partial behavioural viewpoint.

QUALITY CRITERIA

Quality criteria have been discussed for the structure model in Chapter 6 and we may also apply them to the process model. The criteria we discuss are precision, non-complexity and naturalness.

Precision

IE provides some rule types whose semantics are ambiguous. Some examples from the Aquaduct case study are:

- The graphical representations of the minimum and maximum cardinality indicator are the same, where their value is one, as in Figure 11.6 in Chapter 11 (by the Prepare purchase order process). How can they be distinguished?

- The cardinality indicator on a process where it is linked to more than one process via the mutual exclusivity symbol. In this case, it is not clear which process is 'looking across' to this indicator. This is shown in Figure 11.9 in Chapter 11 by the Check customer account monthly process.

- On the process dependency diagram, a process could be shown as dependent on another even where no real world dependency is specified, as in Figure 11.9 in Chapter 11, concerning the Elaborate customer balance process dependency on the Prepare reminder process.

- Single-process iteration is shown by the maximum cardinality indicator of a process having the value N. For example, the process Produce report on transactions in Figures 11.9 and 11.10 in Chapter 11 may be iterated if the report has errors. However, the iteration of a process group may be ambiguous if shown in this way.

Non-complexity

The modelling of iteration may lead to complex diagrams. For example, to specify iteration in MERISE requires a generated event accompanied by a data flow as an initiator of the process that is to be iterated. An example may be seen in Chapter 12, Figure 12.6 for the process Produce report on transactions.

Naturalness

Some of the ways in which the methods group and aggregate concepts seem more suited to designers than to users. For example, all methods use at least one level of process decomposition to reduce the complexity of the model.

Although this can be useful, as it can retain user names for the high- and low-level processes, the technique requires processes to be grouped, and they may be grouped and named into designer processes that do not necessarily correspond to the ways in which users view their processes. Such decomposition is probably more useful as a basis for program refinement and design of procedure-calling sequences.

The methods thus appear to be considering the process hierarchy as a basic organisational viewpoint which users can understand and which enables them to validate diagrams such as DFDs successfully. However, there is growing evidence that such a viewpoint is not the most appropriate for users, and that concepts such as workflow (Dinkhoff *et al.* 1994) or event flow (Flynn and Davarpanah Jazi 1994) may prove more understandable for users when they attempt to validate specifications.

Modelling guidance

In many situations IE provides more than one rule for modelling a given situation. This is a consequence of its powerful set of rules but it requires guidance for making choices that are consistent.

For example, process selection might be modelled with minimum cardinality indicator of zero or using the mutual exclusivity rule, as in Figure 11.9 in Chapter 11 concerning the process Make payment. Another example concerns the representation of one process dependent on several processes, as in Figure 11.3 in Chapter 11, concerning the Send proposal and 1st payment receipt process, where concurrency might also be specified.

CONCLUSIONS

Reference framework

Concepts

There are correspondences between the methods for only two concepts, process and data flow, as shown in Table 13.1.

Viewpoints

There are no complete correspondences between the methods for any of the viewpoints, as shown in Table 13.2. The closest correspondence concerns the data flow viewpoint, but the methods differ with respect to the level of detail provided.

Scope

IE and SSADM have the widest scope of the methods for process modelling, followed by MERISE and MEIN. This is based upon the number and levels of different viewpoints that each method provides.

Quality criteria

Some examples were given where the IE rules would not conform to the precision quality criterion when building a model. Some modelling choice is also required in IE.

It was also observed that the emphasis on the process hierarchy approach to grouping processes may violate the naturalness criterion, and it was felt that no method was particularly suitable for use by an organisational user in this respect.

Part IV

OBJECT-ORIENTED ANALYSIS

Part IV discusses the concepts and diagrams provided by Coad and Yourdon Object-Oriented Analysis (OOA) and then compares the method to the four traditional methods discussed in previous chapters. Both structure and process models are considered.

We discuss structure and process concepts in OOA and then present a partial case study solution, concluding with a method comparison.

Model components

The components of the structure and process models of OOA are as follows:

Structure model	class-&-object layer (diagram)
Process model	class-&-object layer (diagram)
	service chart (diagram)
	object state diagram (diagram)

The service chart and object state diagram make up the class-&-object specification, which also contains a textual element.

Chapter 14

OBJECT-ORIENTED ANALYSIS: STRUCTURE AND PROCESS MODELS

INTRODUCTION

In this chapter we compare the more recent object-oriented approach to analysis by Coad and Yourdon (1991), termed Object-Oriented Analysis (OOA) with the four traditional methods we have considered up until now.

Firstly, we analyse the basic concepts of OOA, using the reference framework that we applied in earlier chapters, describing the OOA structure and process models, and then discuss the reference framework viewpoints. We then look at how a part of the case study is modelled in OOA.

STRUCTURE CONCEPTS

ENTITY

In OOA, the *class-&-object* concept corresponds to the concept of entity.
An *object* is defined as:

> an abstraction of something in a problem domain, reflecting the capabilities of a system to keep information about it or interact with it, or both; an encapsulation of attribute values and their exclusive services

A *class* is defined as:

> a collection of objects which can be described with the same attributes and services

An *object* thus corresponds to our concept of *entity instance* while a *class* corresponds to our concept of *entity type*. The term *instance* is also used by OOA to refer to a given object of a class. The meaning of the term services will be described later. A class is not equivalent to an entity type as the concept of class includes that of services (processes).

Figure 14.1 Object supplier.

Figure 14.2 Class supplier.

Figure 14.3 Class-&-object supplier.

The symbol which graphically represents an object is a soft cornered light rectangle, as shown in Figure 14.1, while the symbol for a class is a soft cornered bold rectangle divided into three sections. Figure 14.2 shows an example of a class.

The name of the class is written in the top section and the section in the middle is provided for the description of the attributes (see below). The third section is used for the services of a class.

A *class-&-object* thus refers to a class and its constituent objects, and it is graphically represented by a class symbol inside an object symbol, as shown in Figure 14.3.

Attribute

In OOA, an attribute is defined as:

> An attribute is some data (state information) for which each object in a class has its own value.

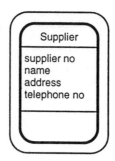

Figure 14.4 *Attributes of class-&-object supplier.*

An attribute is seen as adding detail to a class-&-object and may be single or composite.

Attributes are graphically represented by specifying their names inside their class-&-object symbol under the class-&-object name, as shown in Figure 14.4.

Identifier

OOA regards the decision concerning which, if any, attribute(s) will be an object identifier to be a design-level decision.

Attribute relationship cardinality and optionality

OOA does not provide these.

Binary relationship

OOA provides two concepts which correspond to the binary relationship concept: instance connection and whole-part structure.

Instance connection

This is defined as:

> An instance connection is a model of problem domain mapping(s) that one object needs with other objects, in order to fulfil its responsibilities.

The *instance connection* thus corresponds to the general concept of relationship between entities, as 'instance connections model association'. Implicitly, from OOA examples, it corresponds to a binary but not an *n*-ary relationship.

Graphically, an instance connection is represented by a line drawn between the relevant objects. Figure 14.5 shows a relationship between objects of a single class,

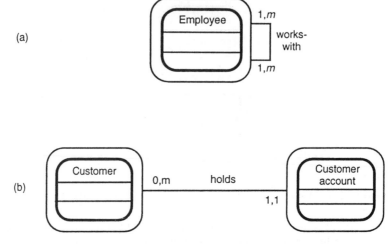

Figure 14.5 Relationships between (a) objects of one class employee, (b) objects of two different classes customer and customer account.

as well as a relationship between objects of two different classes. A relationship name may be specified as shown.

Whole-part structure

Coad and Yourdon suggest that a whole-part structure groups together class-&-objects that are related from one of the following three viewpoints: assembly-parts, container-contents and collection-members.

From the examples given, a *whole-part structure* may be regarded as consisting of one or more typed binary relationships, where a typed binary relationship is a normal binary relationship with the role names 'part of' and 'consists of', from the relevant directions.

The graphical representation of a whole-part structure employs a line drawn between each *whole* and *part* object pair, with a triangle vertex pointing to the *whole* object. An example, shown in Figure 14.6, represents the relationship between department and section, such that a section is part of a department, in the collection-members view. The figure also shows an example representing a part as part of, in the container-contents view, a supplier.

Relationship constraints

OOA provides *range markings* for objects in instance connections and whole-part structures, which correspond to the cardinality and participation constraints. Their

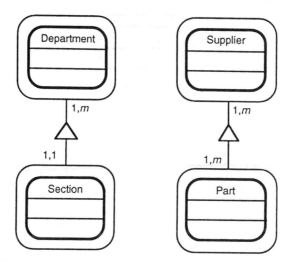

Figure 14.6 *Whole-part structure showing section as part of department and part as part of supplier.*

graphical representation is shown in Figures 14.5 and 14.6 and they are similar to the minimum and maximum cardinality indicators based on the participation style, as in MERISE.

Figure 14.5 represents the situation where an employee must work with many other employees; in addition, a customer may be associated with at least one, and possibly many, customer accounts, with the meaning 'holds', while a customer account must be associated with only one customer.

Figure 14.6 represents the fact that a department must have many 'member' sections, while a section must be part of only one department. A part must be 'part of' many suppliers and a supplier must contain many parts.

Generalisation

OOA provides the *generalisation-specialisation* (*gen-spec*) *structure* which corresponds to the concept of generalisation hierarchy.

A gen-spec structure consists of several class-&-objects arranged in a hierarchy such that a *generalisation class* (supertype) is shown at the top and a *specialisation class* (subtype) is shown at the bottom.

The structure is graphically represented by lines between the relevant classes, with a semi-circle distinguishing the specialisation classes, as shown in Figure 14.7. This represents the situation implied in the case study where customers are classed as existing or potential.

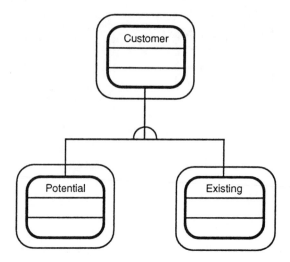

Figure 14.7 *Generalisation–specialisation structure showing potential and existing as specialisations of customer.*

Within the gen-spec structure, property inheritance applies, and specialisation classes can have their specific attributes and services shown, in addition to the more general attributes and services on the generalisation class.

OOA provides a *lattice* structure such that a specialisation class may have more than one generalisation class, inheriting attributes and services from more than one class, thus providing *multiple inheritance*.

Exhaustion may be graphically represented by omitting the object symbol on the generalisation class, implying that it is a class without any directly corresponding objects. *Exclusion* is not modelled.

Summary of structure modelling

The OOA structure modelling concepts are summarised at the end of this chapter.

Figure 14.8 shows an example of structure concepts in OOA, using an excerpt from the Aquaduct case study. This diagram is termed a *layer*, and it is named depending on the concepts it contains. Figure 14.8 shows all concepts except services, and so is termed a class-&-object attribute and structure layer.

The figure shows a gen-spec structure, with potential and existing as specialisations of customer, the whole-part structure supplier:part, class-&-objects customer, customer account and job order showing instance connections between customer and customer account, customer account and job order, part and job order.

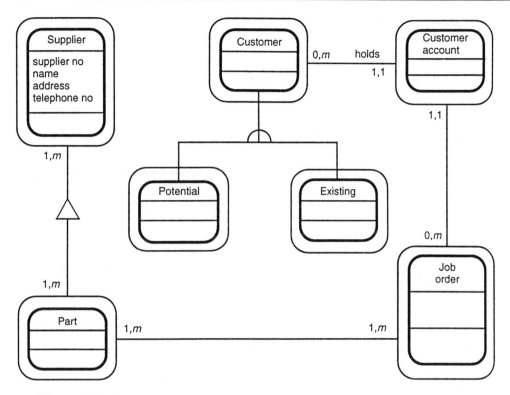

Figure 14.8 *Structure concepts in OOA shown on the class-&-object attribute and structure layer.*

PROCESS CONCEPTS

Introduction

The major difference between OOA and the traditional methods concerns the *object-oriented* nature of the process model. This means that OOA groups processes by the class-&-object affected by those processes.

The reference framework process modelling concepts are: external entity, process, event, data flow, data store and control structure. Of these, OOA provides process, data flow and control structure.

Process

Processes are termed *services* by OOA and are graphically represented on the class-&-object layer as *service names*. A level of refinement of each service is modelled in the *class-&-object specification*, using two diagram types: the *object state diagram* and the *service chart*, which also shows control structure.

Service name

A service is defined thus:

> A service is a specific behaviour that an object is responsible for exhibiting

The name of the service is shown in the bottom section of the class-&-object on which it is grouped, as shown in Figure 14.9, and this name is used for the service chart which describes the service in more detail.

Service chart

The service chart is the main procedural form used for specifying the detail of processes and process control structure. It contains four different components, condition, text block, loop and connector.

Condition

A condition represents certain constraints that have to be met which apply to a process. It corresponds to the concept of *selection*. Graphically, a condition is represented by an irregular hexagonal symbol in which the condition is specified. Figure 14.10 shows an example of a condition.

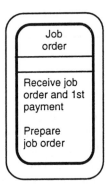

Figure 14.9 Job order class-&-object showing two services: Receive job order and 1st payment and Prepare job order.

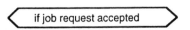

Figure 14.10 A job request is tested for acceptance.

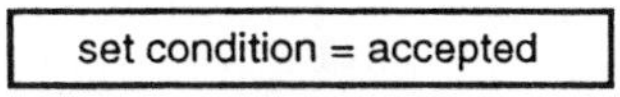

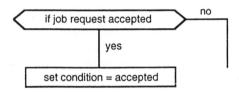

Figure 14.11 Condition is set to accepted.

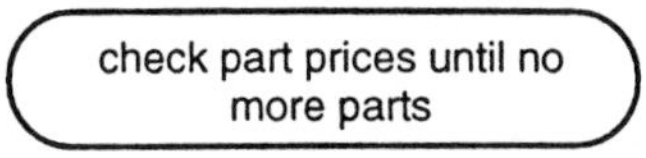

Figure 14.12 Part prices are checked until there are no more parts.

Figure 14.13 If the result from the condition 'if job request accepted' is 'yes' then control passes to 'set condition = accepted'. A 'no' connector is also shown.

Text block

This component specifies a detailed process to be carried out and it is represented by a rectangular box containing the description of the process. Figure 14.11 shows an example.

Loop

A loop represents the repetitive execution of a process under certain constraints. It corresponds to the concept of *iteration*. A loop is graphically represented by a soft-cornered box containing the description of the process and its associated constraint. Figure 14.12 shows an example.

Connector

A connector, represented by a plain line, is used to sequence the loop, text block and condition symbols. It corresponds to the concept of *sequence* and can also be used for *iteration*. Figure 14.13 shows an example. A connector joined to a condition is labelled with 'yes' or 'no'.

Object state diagram

During its lifetime, an object goes through different states until it is not of any more interest to the system. The different states in which an object can exist are

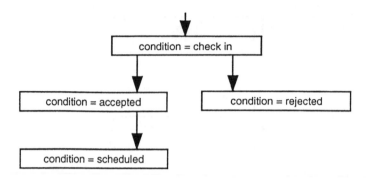

Figure 14.14 *Object state diagram for the job request class-&-object.*

represented by values of the object attributes, changes in which represent changes in state. These are defined in an *object state diagram* which also shows the legal transitions permitted between one state and another.

An object state is represented by a rectangular box inside which the description of the object state is written, in terms of an attribute value or values, and the transition from one state to another is represented by an arrow pointing from one state towards the next legal state. Figure 14.14 shows an example of an object state diagram, where the top arrow represents an initial state. These transitions are specified in the service chart.

Data flow

The *message connection* corresponds to the concept of data flow, and it is a connection between a service of one object and a service of another object. A sender sends a message to a receiver to get some processing done.

The concept is not exactly equivalent to that of data flow as the receiver will take some action and then send a result back to the sender. The message, result and the name of the appropriate service of the receiver is defined in the sender's service chart, while the message, result and required processing are defined in the receiver's service chart.

A message connection is graphically represented by a plain dark shadowed or dashed line with an arrowhead pointing from the object which sends the message, the sender, towards the object or class which receives the message, the receiver. No description is written next to the message connection. Figure 14.15 shows an example.

Figure 14.15 shows that preparing a job proposal entails sending, at some point, a message, and receiving a result, from the part object. The fact that only one service is specified in each object allows us to infer that the message is sent and

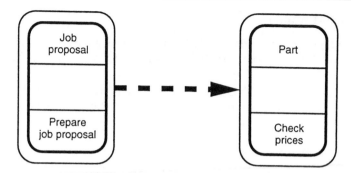

Figure 14.15 *Message connection between job proposal and part.*

received by these services. If there are more services then this diagram would not indicate which services send or receive messages.

Summary of process modelling concepts

The OOA process modelling concepts are summarised at the end of this chapter. We now show part of the Aquaduct case study to illustrate an application of the OOA concepts.

AQUADUCT CASE STUDY IN OOA

Introduction

To illustrate the OOA structure and process models, showing their integrated approach, we use three examples from the Aquaduct case study. We have not used all the case study as these examples are adequate to illustrate the differences between OOA and the traditional approaches.

DFD examples

The first two examples we have chosen focus on the correspondence between the DFD and OOA, and concern the following processes from the DFD shown in Figure 9.3, Chapter 9.

1. Process 1.1 (Receive job request)

2. Process 1.2 (Prepare job order and job proposal) and Process 1.5 (Receive job order and first payment)

MERISE CPM example

The last example concerns the MERISE CPM, and we have chosen the Prepare job order and job proposal operation from the CPM shown in Figure 12.2 in Chapter 12.

To show the features of OOA satisfactorily it is necessary to refine these processes to the next level of detail, and this will be shown in the examples below.

Form of OOA process model

An OOA process model consists of two parts:

1. A class-&-object attribute, structure and service layer containing class-&-objects, showing attributes, structure, message connections and services

2. Class-&-object specifications

The class-&-object specifications consist of a specification for each class-&-object on the class-&-object layer. We present them according to the template in Coad and Yourdon which includes the following elements: attributes, external input/output, object state diagram, additional constraints, service name & service chart.

Aquaduct Example 1 – Receive job request

DFD

This process, shown as process 1.1 Receive job request in Figure 9.3, Chapter 9, is refined into the DFD shown in Figure 14.16. This shows that a job request from a customer is checked in by creating an entry in the job request data store D5. A decision is then made to accept or reject the job request. If the decision is to reject it, the entry in D5 is updated and a rejection letter is sent to the customer. If the decision is to accept it, it is updated to reflect this and then scheduled for later processing.

OOA

The OOA model which corresponds to Figure 14.16 is shown in Figures 14.17–14.19.

Class-&-object, attribute, structure and service layer
Figure 14.17 shows this, which consists of several class-&-objects, and which will be used as a common diagram for both examples. Several of the class-&-objects will

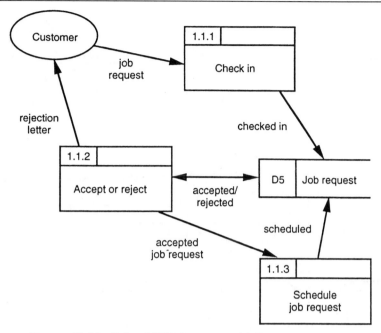

Figure 14.16 Refined DFD for process 1.1 Receive job request.

not be used in the examples, but they are included from previous illustrations to show how the different components interrelate.

For this example, we have made a decision to model a job request by a single class-&-object, job request. One of the main components of the process model, the service name, is shown in this figure, as the job request object has one service name specified, Receive job request.

Class-&-object specifications

Figures 14.18 and 14.19 show the relevant elements of the class-&-object specification for the job request class-&-object. Figure 14.18 shows the attributes of the object as well as one external input (the original job request from the customer).

Two further components of the process model are shown here:

- *Object state diagram.* This shows the legal states and transitions of the attribute condition which represents the states of the job request object. A job request can be in four legal states: check in, accepted, rejected and scheduled.

- *Service chart.* Figure 14.19 shows the service chart for the Receive job request service. When a job request is received, condition is set to 'check in'. A decision is then made concerning the request. If it is to be accepted, then condition is set to 'accepted', the request is scheduled and condition is set to 'scheduled'. If it is to be rejected, condition is set to 'rejected' and a rejection letter is sent.

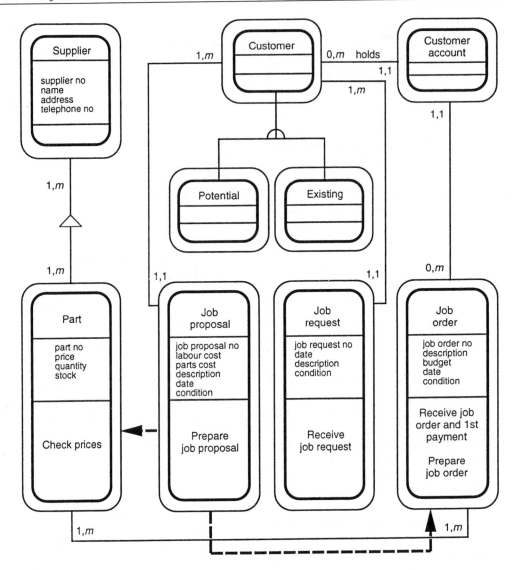

Figure 14.17 *Class-&-object, attribute, structure and service layer.*

Aquaduct Example 2 – Prepare job order and job proposal, receive job order and 1st payment

DFD

Processes 1.2 and 1.5, shown on Figure 9.3, Chapter 9, are refined into the DFDs shown in Figures 14.20 (a) and (b). For the Prepare job order and job proposal

JOB REQUEST SPECIFICATION

attribute	job request number
attribute	date
attribute	description: description of the required job
attribute	condition: the condition of the job request (check in, accepted, rejected, scheduled)
external input	job request details from customer

JOB REQUEST object state diagram

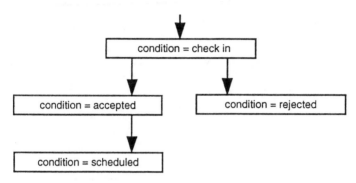

Figure 14.18   Job request specification: attributes, external input and object state diagram.

Receive job request service chart

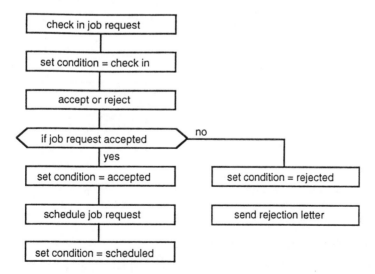

Figure 14.19   Job request specification: Receive job request service chart.

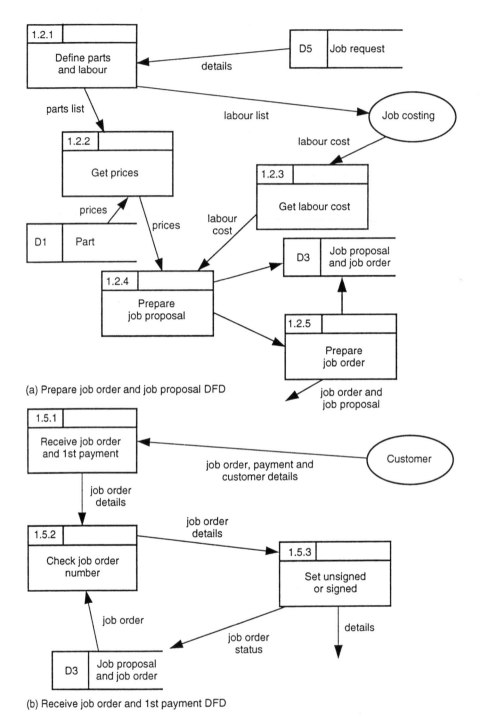

(a) Prepare job order and job proposal DFD

(b) Receive job order and 1st payment DFD

Figure 14.20 Refined DFD for (a) Prepare job order and job proposal process; (b) Receive job order and 1st payment process.

process 1.2, this shows that the first activity is to define the parts and labour required for a particular job request from data store D5. A parts list is produced and then information concerning the prices of those parts is retrieved from the part file. The job costing section receives a labour list and computes the cost of labour required. Finally, a job proposal and a job order are prepared and created on the D3 data store.

For the Receive job order and first payment process 1.5, the job order and payment are received from the customer, the order number is checked and, depending on whether the job order is signed or unsigned the status of the job order is set in the D3 data store.

OOA

The OOA model which corresponds to Figure 14.20 is shown in Figures 14.17 and 14.21–14.23.

Class-&-object, attribute, structure and service layer

Figure 14.17 shows three relevant class-&-objects: job proposal, job order and part, and four corresponding service names: Prepare job proposal, Prepare job order, Receive job order and 1st payment and Check prices.

Two message connections are specified: between job proposal and part and between job proposal and job order.

Class-&-object specifications

Figures 14.21 to 14.23 show the relevant elements of the class-&-object specifications for the three class-&-objects.

(1) *Part*. For the part object, Figure 14.21 shows attributes and an object state diagram (not used by any service). In addition, the service chart for Check prices shows the iteration required when the message is sent from the Prepare job proposal service, asking for prices for parts. After all part prices have been found, the result is returned to the sender. This is also modelled in Figure 14.17 as a message connection between the objects part and job proposal.

(2) *Job proposal*. For the job proposal object, Figure 14.22 shows attributes and an object state diagram. The service chart for Prepare job proposal shows a message is sent to the Check prices service of the part object, asking for prices for parts. It also sends a message to the Prepare job order service of the job order object, asking for a job order to be created. This is also modelled in Figure 14.17 as message connections between the two pairs of objects.

(3) *Job order*. For the job order object, Figures 14.17 and 14.23 show that this object has two services. The Prepare job order service is required to prepare a job order and return a result to the Prepare job proposal service when it is sent a message. It also sets the job order condition to 'prepared'.

PART SPECIFICATION

attribute	part number
attribute	price
attribute	quantity
attribute	stock (available, empty)
external input	part numbers
external output	prices

PART object state diagram

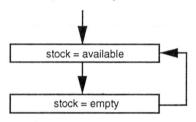

Check prices service chart

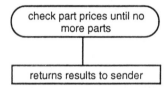

Figure 14.21 Part specification: attributes, object state diagram and service chart.

The Receive job order and 1st payment service checks the job order number and then decides if the job order is signed or unsigned. If unsigned, it sets condition to 'unsigned'; if signed, it sets condition to 'signed'.

Aquaduct Example 3 – Prepare job order and job proposal

MERISE CPM

In order to model a CPM satisfactorily in OOA we have refined the Prepare job order and job proposal operation, from Figure 12.2 in Chapter 12, into a lower-level CPM, and this is shown in Figure 14.24.

This shows that a job request event initiates the operation Define parts and labour. When this is completed the defined parts and labour event occurs, initiating two operations which get part prices and labour costs. When both of these are obtained the Prepare job proposal operation is initiated followed by Prepare job order.

JOB PROPOSAL SPECIFICATION

attribute	job proposal number
attribute	labour ccst
attribute	parts cost
attribute	description
attribute	date
attribute	condition (prepared, accepted, rejected)

JOB PROPOSAL object state diagram

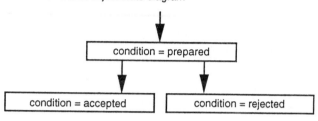

Prepare job proposal service chart

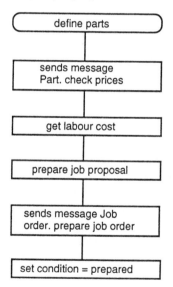

Figure 14.22 *Job proposal specification: attributes, object state diagram and service chart.*

OOA

As this CPM is based on the same process as the DFD in Figure 14.20 (a) the OOA solution will be the same as that shown in Figures 14.21–14.23. However, the CPM provides more direct assistance as it models control structure, providing more of a

JOB ORDER SPECIFICATION

attribute	job order number
attribute	description
attribute	budget
attribute	date
attribute	condition (prepared, unsigned, signed)

JOB ORDER object state diagram

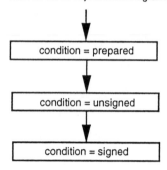

Prepare job order service chart

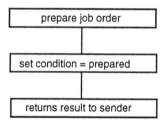

Receive job order and 1st payment service chart

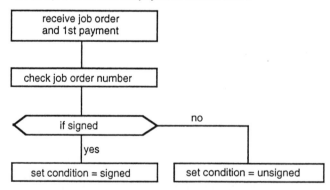

Figure 14.23 Job order specification: attributes, object state diagram, Prepare job order service chart and Receive job order and 1st payment service chart.

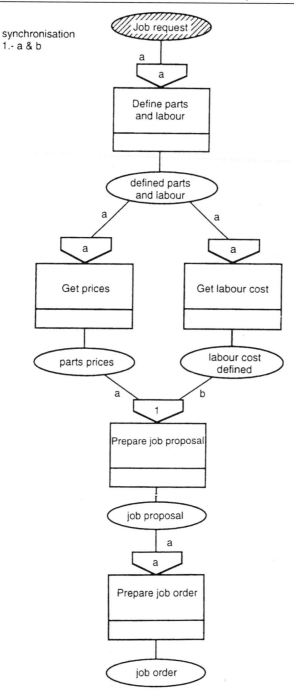

synchronisation
1.- a & b

Figure 14.24 Refined Conceptual Processing Model of Prepare job order and job proposal (MERISE).

correspondence to the service charts, and the internal events may easily correspond to the object state diagram.

SUMMARY

Structure

Table 14.1 shows the structure modelling concepts and their corresponding terms in OOA.

Process

Table 14.2 shows the process concepts and the corresponding terms. Process is modelled, on the highest level, by the service name on the class-&-objects layer.

Table 14.1 Structure modelling concepts and equivalent terms in OOA

Concept	Modelled	Term
		OOA
Entity	yes	class-&-object
Attribute	yes	attribute
Identifier	–	
Attribute relationship cardinality	–	
Attribute relationship optionality	–	
Binary relationship	yes	instance connection, whole-part structure
Cardinality constraint	yes	range markings
Participation constraint	yes	range markings
Relationship attribute	–	
N-ary relationship	–	
Generalisation	yes	gen-spec structure
Property inheritance	yes	inheritance
Multiple inheritance	yes	lattice structure
Exclusion	–	
Exhaustion	yes	
Aggregation	–	
Rule	–	

Table 14.2 Process modelling concepts and equivalent terms in OOA

	OOA	
Concept	**Modelled**	**Term**
External entity	–	
Process	yes	service, text block
Event	–	
Data flow	yes	message connection
Data store	–	
Control structure	yes	condition, loop, connector

Table 14.3 Viewpoints provided by OOA

Viewpoint	**Modelled**
Decomposition	—
Behavioural	class-&-object layer service chart
Data flow	service chart message connection (level 1)
State transition	object state diagram (level 1)

Refinements (one level only) of services are shown on service charts, which also specify process control structure. The object state diagram for an object also shows legal transitions for object states. Data flow is shown by the message connection.

Viewpoints provided

Of the four reference framework viewpoints OOA provides the behavioural, level 1 state transition and level 1 data flow viewpoints. This is shown in Table 14.3.

The decomposition viewpoint is absent as OOA effectively permits only two levels of refinement, service name and service chart. The data flow viewpoint is at level 1 as message connections only specify the objects which send and receive messages, and service charts do not include data stores or external entities. The object state diagram is at level 1 for the state transition viewpoint as no control structure is specified.

Quality criteria

The major difference between the traditional approach and the object oriented approach represented by OOA is the basis for process grouping. This affects the *naturalness* quality criterion, which may concern the need not only for concepts but also for concept relationships to correspond to organisational elements as perceived by the user.

In the traditional approach, processes are decomposed and thereby grouped into a process hierarchy. The basis used for grouping is flexible, which allows processes to be grouped in any suitable way, for example to correspond with the way that users perceive those processes.

In contrast, OOA has a fixed basis for grouping, as processes are grouped on the object affected by those processes.

OOA advantages

An advantage of OOA is that grouping by object is less variable than in the traditional approach, avoiding the problem of flexible grouping.

There may be many different results from flexible grouping. For example, one approach may be to group processes by 'logical unit of work', another may group on the basis that certain processes are all performed by a particular person, while yet another may group on the basis that a set of processes are all performed at the same time. This may confuse users and developers and induce errors.

A further advantage is that an OOA model may map easily to a lower, object-oriented design stage.

OOA disadvantages

A disadvantage of OOA is that grouping by object is inflexible, and may 'split' process specification, resulting in the dismemberment of a group of processes, such as a flow or logical sequence, that is perceived by the user, at variance with the naturalness criterion.

For example, in the case study, we decomposed DFD process 1.2 in Figure 9.3 in Chapter 9 into the process hierarchy shown in Figure 14.20 (a), and the basis we used for grouping was that, in Aquaduct, users perceive these processes as constituting a logical unit of work, as they are executed in a certain sequence and pass related data to one another. Fichman and Kemerer (1992) term this 'end to end' processing.

However, OOA has grouped some of the processes of process 1.2 by object, such as Prepare job proposal and Prepare job order, and thus has split the specification of process 1.2 over those objects.

Although message connections can indicate which processes are linked together, it would be impractical, in a large model, for all such connections to be shown on a class-&-objects layer.

CONCLUSIONS

Reference framework concepts

Correspondences

Table 14.1 shows that for structure, OOA provides entity, attribute, binary relationship, relationship constraints, generalisation, property and multiple inheritance and exhaustion.

For process, Table 14.2 shows that OOA provides process, data flow and control structure.

Differences

For structure, OOA does not provide identifier, attribute relationship constraints, relationship attribute, n-ary relationship, exclusion, aggregation and rule. For process, OOA does not provide external entity, event and data store.

Reference framework viewpoints

Table 14.3 shows that OOA provides three of the four viewpoints.

Quality criteria

The OOA basis for process grouping, whereby processes are grouped by object, was found to conflict with the naturalness criterion, as processes which are viewed as groups by users may be split, making validation difficult.

Comparing OOA and traditional methods

Structure

The OOA structure model is wider in scope than the traditional methods for generalisation-related concepts, but it does not provide concepts such as n-ary relationship and aggregation which some traditional methods have.

Process

The process model does not provide any concepts or viewpoints which are not available in traditional methods. It provides three viewpoints but two of these are only at level 1.

The major difference between OOA and traditional methods is the approach to process grouping, and this means that it is not easy to compare OO and traditional models of the same system. The case study example in this chapter has shown that, due to different process grouping, the process models look totally different. Apart from the ELH of SSADM, traditional method process diagrams are based on flexible process grouping.

General remarks

- OOA process concepts are not as diagrammatically oriented as some traditional methods, which may make user validation difficult

- OOA provides only two levels of process which may make it difficult to build a model for medium or large systems

- An advantage of OOA is that structure and process modelling is, to some extent, integrated. It is unnecessary, as in traditional methods, to map the structure model to data stores

- As OOA provides very detailed specification aids it may be more suited to a lower level of specification concerning developers only, and its model may be more suited to mapping to an object-oriented design stage.

Part V

CONCLUSIONS

In Chapter 15 we draw our conclusions concerning method similarities and differences, method scope, traditional versus object-oriented methods, the uses of the reference framework for training, evaluation and harmonisation, future directions for framework evolution and method convergence, and methods in the future.

Chapter 15

CONCLUSIONS

In this chapter we draw the main conclusions from the comparison of the traditional methods, IE, MEIN, MERISE and SSADM, and the object-oriented OOA of Coad and Yourdon.

METHODS

Structure comparison

Table 15.1 shows the correspondences for structure modelling between the reference framework and the method concepts.

Correspondences

Entity, attribute, binary relationship and relationship cardinality
All methods provide these concepts. MEIN is the only method that does not also provide the other relationship constraint, participation.

Differences

There are significant differences between the methods for the concepts they provide:

1. *Identifier*. This is provided in all methods except OOA, which considers it on the design level.

2. *Attribute relationship cardinality and optionality*. This is not defined at all in MEIN, MERISE or OOA, and is restricted in IE and SSADM.

3. *Relationship attribute*. Relationships with attributes are allowed only by MEIN and MERISE. The other methods use an intersection entity to model this situation, as discussed in Chapter 6.

Table 15.1 Correspondences of structure modelling concepts in IE, MERISE, MEIN, SSADM and OOA

Concept	Method				
	IE	MERISE	MEIN	SSADM	OOA
Entity	yes	yes	yes	yes	yes
Attribute	yes	yes	yes	yes	yes
Identifier	yes	yes	yes	yes	–
Attribute relationship cardinality	yes	–	–	(yes)	–
Attribute relationship optionality	(yes)	–	–	(yes)	–
Binary relationship	yes	yes	yes	yes	yes
Cardinality constraint	yes	yes	yes	yes	yes
Participation constraint	yes	yes	–	yes	yes
Relationship attribute	–	yes	yes	–	–
N-ary relationship	–	yes	yes	–	–
Generalisation	yes	yes	yes	–	yes
Property inheritance	–	yes	yes	–	yes
Multiple inheritance	–	–	–	–	yes
Exclusion	yes	–	–	–	–
Exhaustion	yes	–	–	–	yes
Aggregation	–	–	(yes)	–	–
Rule	–	yes	–	yes	–

4. *N-ary relationship*. Only MEIN and MERISE provide the *n*-ary relationship concept for modelling multiple relationships.

5. *Generalisation*. The coverage of the methods for generalisation varies widely. SSADM only simulates the basic generalisation concept, and OOA, MEIN and MERISE are more extensive since they provide property inheritance. IE is strong on subtype restrictions, providing both exclusion and exhaustion. OOA is the only method to provide multiple inheritance.

6. *Aggregation*. MEIN is the only method to provide this, although it is only partial, allowing a relationship to be treated as an entity.

7. *Rules*. Two of the methods model one rule each, and there is no correspondence between them.

Process comparison

Table 15.2 shows the correspondences between the reference framework concepts for process modelling and the method concepts, while Table 15.3 shows the reference framework viewpoints provided by the process models.

Table 15.2 *Correspondences of process modelling concepts in IE, MERISE, MEIN, SSADM and OOA*

Concept	Method				
	IE	MERISE	MEIN	SSADM	OOA
External entity	–	–	yes	yes	–
Process	yes	yes	yes	yes	yes
Event	yes	yes	–	–	–
Data flow	yes	yes	yes	yes	yes
Data store	yes	–	yes	yes	–
Control structure	yes	(yes)	–	(yes)	yes

Table 15.3 *Correspondences of viewpoints in IE, MERISE, MEIN, SSADM and OOA*

Viewpoint	Method				
	IE	MERISE	MEIN	SSADM	OOA
Decomposition	process decomposition diagram	—	(DFD)	(DFD)	—
Behavioural	process dependency diagram	CPM	—	(ELH)	class-&-object layer service chart
Data flow	process data flow diagram (level 2)	CPM (level 1)	DFD (level 3)	DFD (level 3)	service chart message connection (level 1)
State transition	—	—	—	ELH (level 2)	object state diagram (level 1)

Concepts

Table 15.2 shows that the methods have only two process modelling concepts in common, process and data flow. As we pointed out in Chapter 13 when summarising process modelling, it is necessary to take into account the fact that methods provide particular perspectives or viewpoints, composed of specific concepts and their inter-relationships, and so Table 15.3 is necessary for the comparison, showing the viewpoints each method provides.

Viewpoints

Table 15.3 shows that only one viewpoint, the data flow viewpoint, is provided by all the methods, but they do not all provide it to the same level.

No method corresponds to any other in terms of all the viewpoints provided; instead, we must look for correspondences between viewpoints, rather than between methods.

Data flow

MEIN and SSADM correspond for all concepts they provide in their DFD. The process data flow diagram of IE omits external entities but it may be a subset of a MEIN or SSADM DFD, as long as its control structure is not taken into account.

Data flow in the CPM is restricted to data flow between operations, with no detail provided; in addition, it is not possible to show data flow between different CPMs. This means that it would be difficult to find correspondences to the MERISE CPM from other methods.

State transition

The ELH of SSADM and the object state diagram of OOA may correspond for processes, but not for control structure as the object state diagram does not provide it. For correspondence of models, as opposed to concepts, SSADM entities must be identical to OOA objects.

Behavioural

Both the SSADM ELH and the (class-&-object layer) service name & chart of OOA provide an object-oriented approach to processes and their control structure. Correspondence is partial as the ELH shows only update processes, and correspondence of models would depend on SSADM entities being identical to OOA objects.

The process dependency diagram of IE and the CPM of MERISE may correspond apart from concurrency, which is not provided by the CPM.

Decomposition

If a process hierarchy is abstracted from an SSADM or MEIN DFD then this can be directly compared with an IE process decomposition diagram.

MERISE and OOA only allow two levels of decomposition. For MERISE, this consists of the CPM and the operation, and for OOA it is the service name on the class-&-object layer and the service chart. This limits the level of abstract detail that MERISE and OOA can provide. The main Aquaduct case study was limited to only two levels of detail.

Comparison summary

For structure modelling, all methods use a modelling approach based on entity, attribute and relationship. They differ in their terminology, their graphical representations and the number of concepts they provide and therefore the degree of requirements detail that they can model.

For process modelling, differences are more fundamental, as all methods provide different sets of viewpoints. In addition, the viewpoints of object-oriented methods are all based on a process grouping approach that is different to that of traditional methods.

Method scope

Structure

From Table 15.1, OOA appears to provide the widest scope of structure model, mainly due to its provision of generalisation facilities. However, *n*-ary relationships and aggregation are not allowed. SSADM provides the fewest number of structure modelling concepts.

Process

From Table 15.3, SSADM provides the greatest number of viewpoints, and it is the only method to provide four. However, the fact that it provides only a partial behavioural viewpoint with the ELH should be taken into account. OOA and IE each provide three viewpoints, while MERISE and MEIN provide two each.

It should be noted that if many viewpoints are provided then there is the potential for duplication between different diagrams, leading to possible inconsistencies and extra effort when building and validating the diagrams.

OOA and MERISE may have a problem for medium to large system specification as they only allow two levels of process refinement.

Object-oriented and traditional methods

Although OOA provides a powerful structure model, its process model does not provide any concepts or viewpoints that are not found in other methods. The main difference we found between object-oriented and traditional methods was their approach to process grouping.

Traditional methods seem more suited to a *user* view of the organisation, as they employ flexible process grouping, allowing processes to be grouped in ways that correspond to user perceptions of organisational processes. In contrast, OOA groups processes only on the object that is affected by the processes, and this often has the effect of splitting a group of processes as perceived by the user.

Our first conclusion is that object-oriented grouping is unsuitable for providing a user view of the organisation, as it is too inflexible, but that it may be suitable for a *developer* view of a computer system which will implement the information model. This means that OOA is probably not suitable for the analysis level.

It should be noted that a developer still needs to model the user view of process grouping, as this is required for the design of an integrated social and technical system.

Our second conclusion, for those considering a migration to object-oriented from traditional models, is that such a migration would represent a revolution rather than an evolution, as the two forms of the models, based on different approaches to process grouping, are very different.

REFERENCE FRAMEWORK

The concepts and viewpoints of the reference framework include all the important modelling concepts and viewpoints in the methods considered. The use of the framework in the comparison has established that there are many correspondences between the concepts and viewpoints in different methods, although this is often masked by different terminology and graphical representations.

Framework uses

Education and training

The framework may be used for education and training, as, once the framework terminology, concepts and viewpoints have been acquired, new methods may be learnt easily if they are presented in these terms.

Method evaluation

Another use is to compare the concepts and viewpoints of a method to those of the framework, to establish the scope of a method for an evaluation or procurement exercise. Although there are several factors involved in acquiring a method, such as cost and tool support, the ability of a method to perform information modelling activities is of central importance.

Harmonisation

In Chapter 1 we discussed the harmonisation approach of Euromethod, where an important part of the Method Bridging Guide describes the products of different methods in terms of correspondences to the Deliverables Model concepts. The framework we have discussed is also a possible basis for method harmonisation.

Envisaged procurement process
An example of the way in which our framework might be used in this context concerns the procurement process described in the Preface, where a supplier is tendering to supply a system to a customer using a given method. In this situation, the supplier's tender would describe, in a standard format, the method products to be supplied throughout systems development. Each product description would contain a specification of the correspondences between its concepts and viewpoints and those of the reference framework.

This would assist customer–supplier communication as the products are defined in a standard way.

Questions raised
Two questions are raised by this example:

1. What if there are reference framework concepts or viewpoints that have no correspondences to any of the products of a supplier method?

2. What if there are products of a supplier method that do not correspond to any of the concepts or viewpoints of the reference framework?

The answer to question 1 is that, if the customer insists upon the concept or viewpoint being present in the products, then the supplier must either supplement the method, use a new method or withdraw from the tendering process.

If a method possesses an extra feature then this does not pose a problem, as it may be included in the supplied products, although it is possible that an explanation for it will be required. A supplier could, as a separate exercise, hope to influence the reference framework to include such a feature.

Method convergence

In our view it is likely that methods will converge in the medium term. Firstly, any reference framework will in effect be a 'super-method' as it is likely to be a superset of the most common methods, to avoid the problem of some methods having a wider scope than the reference framework. Although not all customers may insist that a method have correspondences to all of the reference framework, it is possible, with greater awareness of the reference framework, that customers will increasingly demand this where they find it necessary.

For example, if a supplier's method does not provide a state transition viewpoint then increasing customer pressure may force the acquisition of one. The easy, standard choice would probably be the state transition viewpoint defined by the framework.

Secondly, as it may not be possible to avoid expending resources on translating method products into reference framework concepts and viewpoints, a gradual drift of reference framework terminology into methods is likely.

Improvements to our reference framework

Guidance for correct modelling

One respect in which the reference framework is limited is that it does not take into account the fact that there are some modelling situations that require expert choice to select the correct modelling concept, as discussed in Chapter 4 when modelling multiple relationships.

Future work should extend the reference framework, as well as methods, to include modelling guidance concerning the correct choice to be made in such situations.

Modelling guidance – quality criteria

The overall aim of information modelling is to model user requirements completely and correctly. However, it is not enough simply to provide concepts and viewpoints for this, as we also need quality criteria such as precision, non-complexity and naturalness, as discussed in Chapters 4, 6 and 13, to guide the essentially creative information modelling activity where a choice between concepts is required.

We need such guidance to make decisions concerning, for example, whether certain concepts are more complex than others, or whether a certain concept is more or less natural and therefore more or less suitable for model validation.

A direction for further research is to improve the modelling guidance provided in methods, based on quality criteria such as these. The guidance should be related to specific concepts with, if possible, examples of specific modelling situations, which may help to reduce the subjective nature of criteria currently existing. Such guidance may also feature in an extended reference framework.

FUTURE METHODS

Comparing methods and developing standards is not an activity which takes place once and then stops; it is ongoing. The knowledge and experience gained by this type of activity usually leads to insights into the areas of methods that need improvement.

As a result of this study our view is that, typically, methods are *developer-centred* rather than *user-centred* with regard to their products, and this is an area for improvement in future. We saw, for example, that it is often the case that the basis used by developers for grouping and naming processes in process hierarchies is different to that employed by users. Developers may group a set of processes together into a higher-level process and give this 'designer' process a name, which is likely to have little meaning for a user.

It is thus necessary to obtain more insight into the ways in which users actually perceive their organisation, and to reflect this in the techniques used to build models. This particularly true if users are expected to validate and eventually build these models.

One recent approach in this area is discussed in Flynn and Davarpanah Jazi (1994), who argue that users perceive their organisation in terms of *event flows*, each event flow being initiated by an event and comprising related processes, information, actors, objects and organisational structures such as department and section.

Research such as this into new paradigms for constructing models, especially when conducted in organisations in consultation with users, is expected to provide more realistic and effective ways of building models that are more recognisable for users, and which will lead to better quality systems.

Appendix

REFERENCE FRAMEWORK CONCEPTS AND VIEWPOINTS

This appendix lists the reference framework concepts and viewpoints together for convenient reference. The chapter where they are first defined is given.

A *concept* is a 'building block' provided by a method which is used to build an information model. We have not distinguished between concepts which may directly be instantiated to represent organisational elements, such as entity and attribute, and concepts which consist of abstraction operations, such as generalisation and aggregation, that may be performed on instantiable concepts.

A *viewpoint*, defined in Chapter 10, is a perspective over a system consisting of specific concepts and relationships between these concepts.

A viewpoint may be seen as a device to simplify a process model which, if it included every process modelling concept, would be very complex. Methods usually provide several diagrams, where each diagram expresses just one viewpoint.

CONCEPTS

Structure concepts	Chapter
Entity	2
Attribute	2
Identifier	2
Attribute relationship cardinality	2
Attribute relationship optionality	2
Binary relationship	3
Cardinality constraint	3
Participation constraint	3
Relationship attribute	3
N-ary relationship	3 and 4
Generalisation	5

Structure concepts	Chapter
Property inheritance	5
Multiple inheritance	5
Exclusion	5
Exhaustion	5
Aggregation	5
Rule	5

Process concepts	
External entity	8
Process	8
Event	8
Data flow	8
Data store	8
Control structure	10

Viewpoints	
Decomposition	10
Behavioural	10
Data flow	10
State transition	10

REFERENCES

Avison, D. E. and Nandhakumar, J. (1995) The discipline of information systems: let many flowers bloom! *Proceedings of the IFIP International Conference on Information Systems Concepts ISCO3*, March 28–30, Marburg, Germany, 1–21.

Batini, C., Ceri, S. and Navathe, S. B. (1992) *Conceptual database design: an entity-relationship approach*, Benjamin/Cummings, Menlo Park, California.

Benyon, D. (1990) *Information and data modelling*, Blackwell Scientific, Oxford.

Boehm, B. W. (1985) A spiral model of software development and enhancement, *Proceedings of an International Workshop on the Software Process and Software Environments*, Coto de Caza, Trabuco Canyon, California, March 27–9, Wileden, J. C. and Dowson, M. (eds). Reprinted in *ACM SIGSOFT Software Engineering Notes* 11(4), August 1986, 22–42.

Bohm, C. and Jacopini, G. (1966) Flow diagrams, Turing machines and languages with only two formation rules, *Communications of the ACM* 9(5), May, 366–71.

Booch, G. (1991) *Object oriented design: with applications*, Benjamin/Cummings, Menlo Park, California.

British Standards Institute (1987) *BS 5750, Part I: Specification for design/development, production, installation and servicing, Part 2: Guidance.* Available from British Standards Institute, Sales Department, Linford Wood, Milton Keynes, MK14 6LE.

Brodie, M. L. and Silva, E. (1982) Active and passive component modelling: ACM/PCM, in Olle, T. W., Sol, H. G. and Verrijn-Stuart, A. A. (eds), *Information systems design methodologies: a comparative review*, Elsevier, Amsterdam, 41–92.

Bubenko, J. A. (1986) Information system methodologies – a research view, in Olle, T. W., Sol, H. G. and Verrijn-Stuart, A. A. (eds), *Information systems design methodologies: improving the practice*, Elsevier, Amsterdam, 289–318.

CCTA (1994) *Euromethod update, 21 October 1994.* Available from CCTA, Roseberry Court, St Andrews Business Park, Norwich, NR7 0HS, UK.

Checkland, P. (1981) *Systems thinking, systems practice*, Wiley, Chichester.

Chen, P. P. (1976) The entity-relationship model: towards a unified view of data, *ACM Transactions on Database Systems* 1(1), March, 9–36.

Coad, P. (1992) Object-oriented patterns, *Communications of the ACM* 35(9), September, 153–9.

Coad, P. and Yourdon, E. (1991) *Object-oriented analysis*, 2nd edn, Prentice Hall, Englewood Cliffs, NJ.

Collongues, A., Hugues, J. and Laroche, B. (1989) *MERISE 1.– méthode de conception*, DUNOD informatique, Bordas, Paris.

Crinnion, J. (1991) *Evolutionary systems development: a practical guide to the use of prototyping within a structured systems methodology*, Pitman, London.

Daniels, A. and Yeates, D. (1969) *Basic training in systems analysis*, Pitman, London.

De Marco, T. (1979) *Structured analysis and system specification*, Prentice Hall, Englewood Cliffs, NJ.

Dijkstra, E. W. (1968) Go To statement considered harmful, *Communications of the ACM* 11(3), March, 147–8.

Dinkhoff, G., Gruhn, V., Saalmann, A. and Zielonka, M. (1994) Business process modeling in the workflow management environment **Leu**, *Proceedings of the Thirteenth International Conference on Entity-Relationship Approach*, Manchester, UK, 12–14 December, 46–63.

Downs, E., Clare, P. and Coe, I. (1992) *Structured systems analysis and design method*, 2nd edn, Prentice Hall, Hemel Hempstead.

Duschl, R. and Hopkins, N. C. (eds) (1992) *SSADM and GRAPES: two complementary methodologies for information systems engineering*, Springer-Verlag, London.

Eason, K. (1988) *Information technology and organisational change*, Taylor & Francis, London.

EM (1994) *Euromethod version 0*. Available from Euromethod Information Office, Excelsiorlaan 48/50, 1930 Zaventem, Belgium.

Fagan, M. E. (1976) Design and code inspections to reduce errors in program development, *IBM Systems Journal* 15(3), 182–211.

Ferg, S. (1991) Cardinality concepts in entity-relationship modeling, *Proceedings of the Tenth International Conference on Entity-Relationship Approach*, San Mateo, California, 23–5 October, 1–30.

Fichman, R. G. and Kemerer, C. F. (1992) Object-oriented and conventional analysis and design methodologies: comparison and critique, *IEEE Computer*, October, 22–39.

Finkelstein, C. (1989) *An introduction to Information Engineering*, Addison-Wesley, Wokingham.

Flynn, D. J. (1992) *Information systems requirements: determination and analysis*, McGraw-Hill, Maidenhead.

Flynn, D. J. and Arce, E. A. (1995) A CASE tool to support Critical Success Factors analysis in IT planning and requirements determination (*submitted for publication*).

Flynn, D. J. and Davarpanah, Jazi, M. (1994) Event flow diagrams for modelling organizational requirements, *Proceedings of the Thirteenth International Conference on Entity-Relationship Approach*, Manchester, UK, 12–14 December, 79–93.

Flynn, D. J., Vagner, J. and Dal Vecchio, O. (1995) Is CASE technology improving quality and productivity in software development? *Logistics Information Management* 8(2), 8–21.

Franckson, M. (1994) The Euromethod deliverable model and its contribution to the objectives of Euromethod, in Verrijn-Stuart, A. A. and Olle, T. W. (eds), *Methods and associated tools for the information systems life cycle*, Elsevier, Amsterdam, 131–49.

Gane, C. and Sarson, T. (1979) *Structured systems analysis: tools and techniques*, Prentice Hall, Englewood Cliffs, NJ.

Gould, J. D., Boies, S. J. and Lewis, C. (1991) Making usable, useful, productivity-enhancing computer applications, *Communications of the ACM* 34(1), January, 74–85.

Hammer, M. (1990) Reengineering work: don't automate, obliterate! *Harvard Business Review* 68(4), July–August, 104–12.

Hares, J. S. (1990) *SSADM for the advanced practitioner*, Wiley, Chichester.

Harker, S. D. P., Olphert, C. W. and Eason, K. D. (1990) The development of tools to assist in organisational requirements definition for information technology systems, in *Human Computer Interaction INTERACT '90*, Elsevier, Amsterdam.

Hirschheim, R. and Klein, H. K. (1989) Four paradigms of information systems development, *Communications of the ACM* 32(10), October, 1199–216.

Humphrey, W. S. (1989) *Managing the software process*, Addison-Wesley, Reading, MA.

Jackson, M. A. (1975) *Principles of program design*, Academic Press, London.

Jackson, M. A. (1983) *Systems development*, Prentice Hall, Englewood Cliffs, NJ.

Jenkins, T. (ed.) (1992) *Proceedings of the Data Management 92 Conference: 'Systems Development Methods in Europe: 1992 and all that'*, Bristol, 8–9 April. Available from Data Management Specialist Group, British Computer Society, 13 Mansfield Street, London, W1M 0BP.

LBMS (1988) *AUTOMATE PLUS user guide*, Learmonth & Burchett Management Systems, Evelyn House, Oxford Street, London.

Martin, J. (1990) *Information Engineering, Book II: planning and analysis*, Prentice Hall, New York.

Martin, J. and Finkelstein, C. (1981) *Information Engineering*, volume II, Savant Institute, Lancaster, UK.

Martin, J. and McClure, C. (1985) *Diagramming techniques for analysts and programmers*, Prentice Hall, New York.

MEIN II (1991) Entorno metodologico: analysis functional version 1, reference manual, ERITEL, Madrid, Spain.

Mumford, E. (1983) *Designing human systems for new technology: the ETHICS method*, Manchester Business School, Manchester.

Nijssen, G. M. and Halpin, T. A. (1989) *Conceptual schema and relational database design: a fact oriented approach*, Prentice Hall, Sydney.

Olle, T. W., Hagelstein, J., Macdonald, I. G., Roland, C., Sol, H. G., Van Assche, F. J. M. and Verrijn-Stuart, A. A. (eds) (1988) *Information systems methodologies: a framework for understanding*, Addison-Wesley, Wokingham.

Olle, T. W., Sol, H. G. and Tully, C. J. (eds) (1983) *Information systems design methodologies: a feature analysis*, North-Holland, Amsterdam.

Olle, T. W., Sol, H. G. and Verrijn-Stuart, A. A. (eds) (1982) *Information systems design methodologies: a comparative review*, North-Holland, Amsterdam.

Olle, T. W., Sol, H. G. and Verrijn-Stuart, A. A. (eds) (1986) *Information systems design methodologies: improving the practice*, North-Holland, Amsterdam.

Parnas, D. L. (1972) A technique for software module specification with examples, *Communications of the ACM* 15(5), May, 330–6.

Planche, R. (1992) *Data driven systems modelling*, Prentice Hall/Masson, Paris.

Quang, P. T. and Chartier-Kastler, C. (1991) *MERISE in practice (translated by D. and M.-A. Avison)*, Macmillan, London.

Quintas, P. (1994) A product-process model of innovation in software development, *Journal of Information Technology* 9, 3–17.

Ramesh, B. and Luqi (1993) Process knowledge based rapid prototyping for requirements engineering, *Proceedings of the IEEE International Symposium on Requirements Engineering*, 4–6 January, San Diego, California, 248–55.

Rochfeld, A. (1987) MERISE, an information system design and development methodo-logy, in Spaccapietra, S. (ed.), *Entity-Relationship Approach*, Elsevier, Amsterdam, 489–528.

Rochfeld, A. and Tardieu, H. (1983) MERISE: an information system design and development methodology, *Information Management* 6(3), 143–59.

Rumbaugh, J., Blaha, M., Premeriani, W., Eddy, F. and Lorensen, W. (1991) *Object-oriented modeling and design*, Prentice Hall, Englewood Cliffs, NJ.

Shlaer, S. and Mellor, S. J. (1988) *Object-oriented systems analysis: modeling the world in data*, Prentice Hall, Englewood Cliffs, NJ.

Singh, R. (1994) ISO/IEC draft international standard 12207, software life-cycle processes, in Verrijn-Stuart, A. A. and Olle, T. W. (eds), *Methods and associated tools for the information systems life cycle*, Elsevier, Amsterdam, 111–19.

Smith, J. M. and Smith, D. C. P. (1977) Database abstractions: aggregation and generaliza-tion, *ACM Transactions on Database Systems* 2(2), June, 105–33.

SSADM (1990) *Version 4 Reference Manual*, 4 volumes, NCC Blackwell, Oxford.

Stevens, W., Myers, G. and Constantine, L. (1974) Structured design, *IBM Systems Journal* 13(2), May, 115–39.

Tardieu, H., Rochfeld, A. and Colletti, R. (1983) *La méthode MERISE - principes et outils*, tome 1, Les éditions d'Organisation, Paris.

Tardieu, H., Rochfeld, A., Colletti, R., Panet, G. and Vahee, G. (1985) *La méthode MERISE - principes et outils*, tome 2, Les éditions d'Organisation, Paris.

Ter Bekke, J. H. (1992) *Semantic data modelling*, Prentice Hall, Hemel Hempstead.

TickIT (1992) *TickIT. Guide to software quality management system construction and certification using ISO 9001/EN29001/BS 5750 Part 1, Issue 2.0*, Department of Trade and Industry, Department for Enterprise, London.

Tsichritzis, D. and Lochovsky, F. H. (1982) *Data models*, Prentice Hall, Englewood Cliffs, NJ.

Verrijn-Stuart, A. A. and Olle, T. W. (eds) (1994) *Methods and associated tools for the information systems life cycle*, Elsevier, Amsterdam.

Warnier, J.-D. (1974) *Logical construction of programs*, Van Nostrand Rheinhold, New York.

Wintraecken, J. J. V. R. (1990) *The NIAM information analysis method: theory and practice*, Kluwer Academic, Utrecht.

Yourdon, E. and Constantine, L. L. (1979) *Structured design: fundamentals of a discipline of computer program and systems design*, Prentice Hall, Englewood Cliffs, NJ.

Yu, E.S.K. (1993) Modelling organizations for information systems requirements engineer-ing, *Proceedings of the IEEE International Symposium on Requirements Engineering*, 4–6 January, San Diego, California, 34–41.

INDEX